50 Easy Meals To cook

By D.C.V

- Spaghetti Aglio e Olio
- Grilled Cheese Sandwich
- Vegetable Stir-Fry
- Quesadillas
- Tomato Soup with Grilled Cheese Croutons
- Omelette with Spinach and Cheese
- Fried Rice
- Pasta Primavera
- Caprese Salad (Tomato, Mozzarella, Basil)
- Tacos (with your choice of filling)
- Baked Chicken Breasts with Steamed Vegetables
- Stir-Fried Noodles with Vegetables
- Margherita Pizza
- Lentil Soup
- Baked Salmon with Lemon and Dill
- BLT Sandwich (Bacon, Lettuce, Tomato)
- Veggie Omelette
- Beef or Veggie Burgers
- Chicken Caesar Salad
- Chili Con Carne
- Pesto Pasta
- Grilled Chicken with Roasted Vegetables
- Ratatouille
- Teriyaki Chicken with Rice
- Greek Salad with Grilled Chicken

- Tuna Salad Sandwich
- Spinach and Feta Stuffed Chicken Breast
- Shrimp Stir-Fry
- Vegetable Curry
- Bruschetta with Tomato and Basil
- Beef Stew
- Baked Ziti
- Lemon Garlic Shrimp Pasta
- Chicken Fajitas
- Roasted Vegetable Quinoa Bowl
- Pan-Seared Steak with Mashed Potatoes
- Stuffed Bell Peppers
- Chicken and Broccoli Stir-Fry
- Thai Peanut Noodles
- BBQ Chicken Pizza
- Veggie Burrito Bowl
- Mushroom Risotto
- Sautéed Garlic Butter Shrimp
- Turkey Chili
- Falafel with Tzatziki Sauce
- Hawaiian Chicken Skewers
- Beef and Broccoli Stir-Fry
- Sweet Potato and Black Bean Quesadillas
- Chicken Piccata
- Veggie Frittata

Spaghetti Aglio e Olio

Spaghetti Aglio e Olio

Ingredients:
- 8 oz (225g) spaghetti
- 4 cloves garlic, thinly sliced
- 1/4 cup (60ml) extra virgin olive oil
- 1/2 teaspoon red pepper flakes (adjust to taste)
- Salt, to taste
- Freshly ground black pepper, to taste
- Fresh parsley, chopped, for garnish
- Grated Parmesan cheese, for serving (optional)

Instructions:
1. Cook the Pasta:
   - Bring a large pot of salted water to a boil.
   - Cook the spaghetti according to the package instructions until al dente.
   - Reserve about 1/2 cup of pasta water before draining the spaghetti.
2. Prepare the Garlic Infused Oil:
   - While the pasta is cooking, heat the olive oil in a large skillet over medium heat.
   - Add the sliced garlic and red pepper flakes to the skillet.
   - Cook, stirring frequently, for about 2-3 minutes, or until the garlic is lightly golden and fragrant. Be careful not to let it burn.
3. Combine Pasta and Garlic Oil:
   - Once the spaghetti is cooked, add it directly to the skillet with the garlic oil.
   - Toss the spaghetti in the oil until well coated, adding a splash of pasta water if needed to loosen the sauce and prevent sticking.
   - Season generously with salt and pepper to taste.
4. Serve:
   - Transfer the spaghetti aglio e olio to serving plates or bowls.
   - Garnish with chopped fresh parsley.
   - Optionally, sprinkle grated Parmesan cheese on top before serving for added flavor.
5. Enjoy!
   - Serve the spaghetti aglio e olio immediately while hot, savoring the simple yet delicious flavors of garlic-infused olive oil with a hint of heat from the red pepper flakes.

This dish is perfect for when you're short on time but still want a satisfying and flavorful meal. Pair it with a crisp salad and some crusty bread for a complete dining experience. Buon appetito!

Grilled Cheese Sandwich

Grilled Cheese Sandwich

Ingredients:
- 4 slices of bread (sourdough, whole wheat, or your choice)
- 2 cups shredded cheese (Cheddar, American, Swiss, or a mix)
- 2 tablespoons butter, softened
- 1 tablespoon mayonnaise (optional, for added flavor and crispiness)
- Optional add-ins: sliced tomatoes, cooked bacon, caramelized onions, avocado slices, etc.

Instructions:
1. Preheat the Pan:
   - Place a non-stick skillet or griddle over medium-low heat to preheat.
2. Assemble the Sandwich:
   - Spread a thin layer of butter on one side of each slice of bread. If using mayonnaise, spread it on the other side of each slice.
   - Place a handful of shredded cheese on the unbuttered side of two bread slices.
   - If desired, add any optional add-ins on top of the cheese.
   - Top each with another slice of bread, buttered side facing outwards.
3. Grill the Sandwich:
   - Carefully place the assembled sandwiches onto the preheated skillet or griddle.
   - Cook for 3-4 minutes on each side, or until the bread is golden brown and crispy, and the cheese is melted.
4. Serve:
   - Once both sides are golden and the cheese is melted, transfer the grilled cheese sandwiches to a cutting board.
   - Let them cool for a minute or two before slicing diagonally.
   - Serve hot with your favorite dipping sauce or a side of tomato soup for dipping.
5. Enjoy!

Vegetable Stir-Fry

Vegetable Stir-Fry

Ingredients:
- 2 tablespoons vegetable oil
- 2 cloves garlic, minced
- 1-inch piece of ginger, minced
- 1 onion, thinly sliced
- 2 bell peppers, thinly sliced (any color)
- 2 carrots, julienned
- 1 cup broccoli florets
- 1 cup snap peas or snow peas, trimmed
- 1 cup sliced mushrooms (such as button or shiitake)
- 1 cup sliced cabbage
- 1/4 cup soy sauce
- 2 tablespoons oyster sauce (optional)
- 1 tablespoon sesame oil
- 1 tablespoon cornstarch (optional, for thickening sauce)
- Cooked rice or noodles, for serving

Instructions:
1. Prepare the Sauce:
   - In a small bowl, whisk together the soy sauce, oyster sauce (if using), sesame oil, and cornstarch (if using). Set aside.
2. Heat the Wok or Skillet:
   - Heat the vegetable oil in a large wok or skillet over medium-high heat.
3. Cook the Aromatics:
   - Add the minced garlic and ginger to the hot oil.
   - Stir-fry for about 30 seconds until fragrant, being careful not to burn them.
4. Add the Vegetables:
   - Add the sliced onion to the wok and stir-fry for 1-2 minutes until it starts to soften.
   - Add the bell peppers, carrots, broccoli, snap peas, mushrooms, and cabbage to the wok.
   - Stir-fry the vegetables for 3-4 minutes until they are tender-crisp but still vibrant in color.
5. Add the Sauce:
   - Pour the sauce mixture over the vegetables in the wok.
   - Stir well to coat the vegetables evenly with the sauce.
   - Cook for an additional 1-2 minutes until the sauce thickens slightly and coats the vegetables.
6. Serve:
   - Remove the wok from the heat.
   - Serve the vegetable stir-fry hot over cooked rice or noodles.
   - Garnish with sliced green onions or sesame seeds if desired.
7. Enjoy!

Quesadillas

Quesadillas

Ingredients:
- Flour tortillas (8-inch size works well)
- Shredded cheese (common choices include cheddar, Monterey Jack, or a Mexican cheese blend)
- Cooked protein (such as grilled chicken, steak strips, shrimp, or seasoned ground beef)
- Optional fillings: sliced bell peppers, onions, mushrooms, black beans, corn kernels, diced tomatoes, jalapeños, etc.
- Optional seasonings: cumin, chili powder, garlic powder, paprika, etc.
- Cooking oil or butter, for frying

Instructions:
1. Prepare Fillings:
   - If you're using any raw vegetables, sauté them lightly until they're just tender. Season with salt, pepper, and any desired spices.
   - Cook the protein if it's not already cooked. Season with your preferred spices for extra flavor.
2. Assemble Quesadillas:
   - Lay one tortilla flat on a clean surface.
   - Sprinkle a generous amount of shredded cheese evenly over one half of the tortilla, leaving some space around the edges.
   - Add your desired fillings on top of the cheese. Be careful not to overfill, as it might make folding difficult.
   - Sprinkle a bit more cheese on top to help everything stick together.
3. Fold and Cook:
   - Fold the empty half of the tortilla over the filling to create a half-moon shape.
   - Heat a non-stick skillet or griddle over medium heat. Add a small amount of oil or butter to the pan.
   - Carefully transfer the assembled quesadilla to the skillet and cook until the bottom is golden brown and crispy, about 2-3 minutes.
4. Flip and Finish Cooking:
   - Carefully flip the quesadilla using a spatula and cook the other side until it's golden brown and the cheese is melted.
   - Press down lightly with the spatula while cooking to help the ingredients stick together.
5. Serve:
   - Once both sides are nicely browned and the cheese is melted, remove the quesadilla from the skillet and place it on a cutting board.
   - Let it cool for a minute or two, then slice it into wedges using a sharp knife or pizza cutter.
   - Serve hot with your favorite toppings and dipping sauces, such as salsa, guacamole, sour cream, or hot sauce.

Feel free to customize your quesadillas with different fillings, spices, and toppings to suit your taste preferences. They're perfect for a quick and satisfying meal or snack any time of day!

Tomato Soup with Grilled Cheese Croutons

Tomato Soup with Grilled Cheese Croutons

Tomato Soup Ingredients:
- 2 tablespoons olive oil
- 1 onion, diced
- 2 cloves garlic, minced
- 2 cans (28 ounces each) whole peeled tomatoes
- 2 cups vegetable or chicken broth
- 1 teaspoon dried basil
- 1 teaspoon dried oregano
- 1/2 teaspoon dried thyme
- Salt and pepper, to taste
- 1/2 cup heavy cream (optional, for added richness)
- Fresh basil leaves, for garnish (optional)

Grilled Cheese Croutons Ingredients:
- 4 slices of bread (any type you prefer)
- Butter, softened
- Cheese slices (cheddar, Swiss, or your favorite melting cheese)
- Instructions:

Tomato Soup:
1. Sauté Aromatics:
    - In a large pot or Dutch oven, heat the olive oil over medium heat. Add the diced onion and cook until softened, about 5 minutes. Add the minced garlic and cook for another 1-2 minutes until fragrant.
2. Simmer Soup:
    - Pour in the canned tomatoes with their juices and the vegetable or chicken broth. Stir in the dried basil, dried oregano, and dried thyme. Season with salt and pepper to taste.
    - Bring the soup to a simmer and let it cook for about 15-20 minutes, stirring occasionally, to allow the flavors to meld together.
3. Blend Soup (Optional):
    - If you prefer a smoother consistency, use an immersion blender to puree the soup directly in the pot until smooth. Alternatively, you can transfer the soup in batches to a blender and blend until smooth, then return it to the pot.
4. Finish Soup:
    - Stir in the heavy cream, if using, to add richness to the soup. Taste and adjust seasoning as needed.

Grilled Cheese Croutons:
1. Assemble Sandwiches:
    - Preheat a skillet or griddle over medium heat. Butter one side of each bread slice.
    - Place the bread slices buttered side down on a clean surface. Add a slice of cheese to each slice of bread, then top with another slice of bread, buttered side up, to form sandwiches.
2. Grill Sandwiches:
    - Place the sandwiches on the preheated skillet or griddle. Cook until the bottom is golden brown and the cheese starts to melt, about 2-3 minutes.
    - Flip the sandwiches and continue to cook until the other side is golden brown and the cheese is completely melted, another 2-3 minutes.
3. Cut into Croutons:
    - Remove the sandwiches from the skillet and let them cool slightly. Use a sharp knife to cut each sandwich into bite-sized squares or triangles, creating grilled cheese croutons.

Serve:
- Ladle the hot tomato soup into bowls. Top each bowl with a handful of grilled cheese croutons.
- Garnish with fresh basil leaves, if desired.
- Serve immediately and enjoy your comforting bowl of tomato soup with grilled cheese croutons!

Feel free to adjust the seasonings and add your favorite herbs or spices to customize the soup to your taste. It's a classic combination that's sure to warm you up from the inside out!

Omelette with Spinach and Cheese

Omelette with Spinach and Cheese

Ingredients:
- 3 large eggs
- 1 cup fresh spinach leaves, washed and chopped
- 1/4 cup shredded cheese (such as cheddar, mozzarella, or feta)
- Salt and pepper, to taste
- 1 tablespoon butter or cooking oil

Optional Additions:
- Diced onions
- Sliced mushrooms
- Diced bell peppers
- Diced tomatoes
- Cooked bacon or ham
- Fresh herbs (such as parsley or chives)

Instructions:
1. Prepare Ingredients:
   - Crack the eggs into a bowl and beat them lightly with a fork or whisk until well combined. Season with a pinch of salt and pepper.
   - Wash the spinach leaves thoroughly and chop them into small pieces. If you're using any additional ingredients like onions, mushrooms, or bell peppers, prepare them as well.
2. Heat Pan:
   - Heat a non-stick skillet over medium heat. Add the butter or cooking oil and let it melt and coat the bottom of the pan.
3. Cook Spinach:
   - Once the butter is melted and the pan is hot, add the chopped spinach to the skillet. Cook for 1-2 minutes, stirring occasionally, until the spinach is wilted and slightly softened. If you're using any other vegetables, you can sauté them along with the spinach.
4. Pour in Eggs:
   - Pour the beaten eggs over the cooked spinach in the skillet. Use a spatula to gently stir the eggs and spinach mixture, allowing the uncooked eggs to flow to the bottom of the pan.
5. Add Cheese:
   - Once the eggs start to set on the bottom and around the edges, sprinkle the shredded cheese evenly over the top of the omelette.
6. Fold Omelette:
   - Using a spatula, carefully lift one side of the omelette and fold it over the other side to form a half-moon shape. Press down gently with the spatula to seal the omelette.
7. Cook Until Set:
   - Let the omelette cook for another 1-2 minutes, or until the cheese is melted and the eggs are fully set. You can gently press down on the omelette with the spatula to ensure it's cooked through.
8. Serve:
   - Slide the cooked omelette onto a plate. You can garnish it with additional cheese, chopped herbs, or a sprinkle of black pepper if desired.
   - Serve hot and enjoy your delicious omelette with spinach and cheese!

Feel free to customize your omelette with your favorite ingredients and experiment with different cheese and vegetable combinations. It's a versatile dish that's quick and easy to make, yet satisfying and packed with flavor!

Fried Rice

Fried Rice

Ingredients:
- 2 cups cooked rice (preferably day-old rice, as it fries up better)
- 2 tablespoons cooking oil (such as vegetable oil or sesame oil)
- 2 cloves garlic, minced
- 1 small onion, finely chopped
- 1 cup mixed vegetables (such as diced carrots, peas, corn, bell peppers, and green beans)
- 2 eggs, lightly beaten
- 2 tablespoons soy sauce
- Salt and pepper, to taste
- Optional garnishes: chopped green onions, sliced scallions, sesame seeds

Optional Additions:
- Diced cooked chicken, shrimp, or tofu
- Sliced mushrooms
- Bean sprouts
- Chopped cilantro or parsley
- Diced ham or bacon
- Pineapple chunks

Instructions:
1. Prepare Ingredients:
   - If you're using day-old rice, break up any clumps with your fingers to separate the grains. If you're using freshly cooked rice, spread it out on a baking sheet to cool and dry slightly.
   - Mince the garlic, chop the onion, and prepare any other vegetables or protein you'll be using.
2. Heat Oil:
   - Heat the cooking oil in a large skillet or wok over medium-high heat. Make sure the pan is hot before adding the ingredients.
3. Sauté Aromatics:
   - Add the minced garlic and chopped onion to the hot oil. Sauté for 1-2 minutes until the onions are translucent and fragrant.
4. Add Vegetables:
   - Add the mixed vegetables to the skillet. Stir-fry for 3-4 minutes until they are tender-crisp. If you're using any raw meat or tofu, you can add it at this stage and cook until it's no longer pink or raw.
5. Scramble Eggs:
   - Push the vegetables to one side of the skillet to create a space for the eggs. Pour the beaten eggs into the empty space. Let them cook for a few seconds until they start to set, then scramble them with a spatula until they're fully cooked and scrambled.
6. Combine with Rice:
   - Add the cooked rice to the skillet, breaking up any clumps with a spatula. Stir-fry everything together, mixing well to distribute the eggs and vegetables evenly throughout the rice.
7. Season with Soy Sauce:
   - Drizzle the soy sauce over the rice mixture, tossing continuously to coat everything evenly. Season with salt and pepper to taste. Adjust the amount of soy sauce according to your preference.
8. Finish and Garnish:
   - Continue to cook the fried rice for another 2-3 minutes, stirring occasionally, until everything is heated through and well combined.
   - Remove the skillet from heat. Taste and adjust seasoning if needed. Sprinkle chopped green onions, sliced scallions, or sesame seeds on top for garnish, if desired.
9. Serve:
   - Transfer the fried rice to serving plates or bowls. Serve hot as a main dish or side dish alongside your favorite Asian-inspired dishes.

Enjoy your homemade fried rice, and feel free to customize it with your favorite ingredients to make it your own signature dish

Pasta Primavera

Pasta Primavera

Ingredients:
- 12 ounces pasta (such as fettuccine, spaghetti, or penne)
- 2 tablespoons olive oil
- 3 cloves garlic, minced
- 1 small onion, thinly sliced
- 1 cup cherry tomatoes, halved
- 1 cup broccoli florets
- 1 cup sliced bell peppers (mix of colors for visual appeal)
- 1 cup sliced carrots
- 1 cup sliced zucchini or yellow squash
- Salt and pepper, to taste
- 1/2 cup heavy cream (optional, for a creamy sauce)
- 1/4 cup grated Parmesan cheese, plus extra for serving
- Fresh basil or parsley, chopped, for garnish

Instructions:
1. Prepare Pasta:
   - Cook the pasta according to the package instructions in a large pot of salted boiling water until al dente. Drain the cooked pasta and set aside. Reserve about 1/2 cup of pasta cooking water.
2. Sauté Vegetables:
   - Heat the olive oil in a large skillet over medium heat. Add the minced garlic and sliced onion, and sauté for 2-3 minutes until fragrant and softened.
   - Add the cherry tomatoes, broccoli florets, sliced bell peppers, sliced carrots, and sliced zucchini or yellow squash to the skillet. Season with salt and pepper to taste. Cook, stirring occasionally, for 5-7 minutes until the vegetables are tender-crisp.
3. Combine Pasta and Vegetables:
   - Add the cooked pasta to the skillet with the sautéed vegetables. Toss everything together gently to combine.
4. Add Cream and Cheese (Optional):
   - If using, pour the heavy cream into the skillet and stir to coat the pasta and vegetables evenly. Cook for an additional 1-2 minutes until the cream is heated through.
   - Sprinkle grated Parmesan cheese over the pasta primavera and toss to combine. If the sauce seems too thick, you can add some of the reserved pasta cooking water to loosen it up.
5. Garnish and Serve:
   - Remove the skillet from heat. Taste and adjust seasoning if needed, adding more salt and pepper if desired.
   - Garnish the pasta primavera with chopped fresh basil or parsley for a burst of flavor and color.
   - Serve hot, portioned into bowls or plates, with additional grated Parmesan cheese on the side for sprinkling.

Enjoy your vibrant and flavorful Pasta Primavera as a main course or side dish. It's a wonderful way to celebrate the bounty of spring vegetables and indulge in a satisfying pasta meal!

Caprese Salad (Tomato, Mozzarella, Basil)

Caprese Salad (Tomato, Mozzarella, Basil)

Ingredients:
- 2 large ripe tomatoes
- 8 ounces fresh mozzarella cheese
- Fresh basil leaves
- Extra virgin olive oil
- Balsamic glaze or balsamic vinegar (optional)
- Salt and pepper, to taste

Instructions:
1. Prepare Ingredients:
   - Wash the tomatoes and basil leaves. Pat them dry with a paper towel.
   - Slice the tomatoes and fresh mozzarella cheese into rounds, about 1/4 inch thick.
2. Assemble Salad:
   - On a serving platter or individual plates, alternate slices of tomato and mozzarella cheese.
   - Tuck fresh basil leaves between the tomato and cheese slices. You can use whole leaves or tear them into smaller pieces.
3. Season and Drizzle:
   - Drizzle extra virgin olive oil over the assembled salad.
   - Season with salt and pepper to taste.
4. Optional Balsamic Glaze:
   - If desired, drizzle balsamic glaze or balsamic vinegar over the salad for added flavor. This step is optional but adds a nice tangy sweetness to the dish.
5. Serve:
   - Serve the Caprese Salad immediately as a refreshing appetizer or side dish.
   - Enjoy it with crusty bread to soak up the delicious juices, or alongside grilled meats for a complete meal.

Caprese Salad is best enjoyed when the ingredients are fresh and at room temperature. It's a perfect dish for showcasing the flavors of summer and is sure to be a hit at any gathering!

-

Tacos (with your choice of filling)

Tacos (with your choice of filling)

Ingredients:
- 8-10 small corn or flour tortillas
- Your choice of filling options:
    - Grilled chicken, beef, pork, shrimp, fish, or tofu
    - Seasoned ground beef or turkey
    - Sauteed or grilled vegetables (bell peppers, onions, mushrooms, zucchini, etc.)
    - Refried beans or black beans
- Toppings:
    - Shredded lettuce or cabbage
    - Diced tomatoes
    - Diced onions
    - Sliced avocado or guacamole
    - Shredded cheese (cheddar, Monterey Jack, or Mexican blend)
    - Chopped cilantro
    - Sour cream or Greek yogurt
    - Salsa or hot sauce
- Lime wedges, for serving
- Salt and pepper, to taste
- Cooking oil (if needed for cooking the filling)

Instructions:
1. Prepare Fillings:
    - Cook your choice of filling according to your preference. For example, grill or sauté chicken, beef, shrimp, or tofu until cooked through and season with your favorite spices. If using ground meat, cook it with onions, garlic, and taco seasoning until browned and flavorful. If using beans, heat them on the stove until warmed through.
    - Prepare any additional toppings and set them aside in separate bowls.
2. Warm Tortillas:
    - Heat a non-stick skillet or griddle over medium heat. Warm the tortillas in the skillet for about 30 seconds on each side until they are soft and pliable. Alternatively, you can warm them in the microwave wrapped in a damp paper towel for about 30 seconds.
3. Assemble Tacos:
    - Place a spoonful of your chosen filling in the center of each tortilla.
    - Top with your desired toppings, such as shredded lettuce, diced tomatoes, onions, avocado slices, cheese, cilantro, sour cream, and salsa.
    - Squeeze a fresh lime wedge over each taco for a burst of citrus flavor.
    - Season with salt and pepper to taste.

Baked Chicken Breasts with Steamed Vegetables

Baked Chicken Breasts with Steamed Vegetables

Ingredients:
- 4 boneless, skinless chicken breasts
- 2 tablespoons olive oil
- 2 cloves garlic, minced
- 1 teaspoon paprika
- 1 teaspoon dried thyme
- 1 teaspoon dried rosemary
- Salt and pepper, to taste
- 4 cups mixed vegetables (such as broccoli florets, carrots, cauliflower, and green beans)
- Lemon wedges, for serving (optional)
- Fresh parsley, chopped, for garnish (optional)

Instructions:

1. Preheat Oven:
   - Preheat your oven to 400°F (200°C).
2. Prepare Chicken:
   - Place the chicken breasts on a cutting board. Pat them dry with paper towels.
   - In a small bowl, combine the olive oil, minced garlic, paprika, dried thyme, dried rosemary, salt, and pepper. Stir to form a marinade.
   - Rub the marinade evenly over both sides of the chicken breasts.
3. Bake Chicken:
   - Place the seasoned chicken breasts in a baking dish or on a baking sheet lined with parchment paper.
   - Bake in the preheated oven for 20-25 minutes, or until the chicken is cooked through and reaches an internal temperature of 165°F (75°C). Cooking time may vary depending on the thickness of the chicken breasts.
4. Prepare Vegetables:
   - While the chicken is baking, prepare the mixed vegetables. Wash and chop the vegetables into bite-sized pieces.
   - Place the chopped vegetables in a steamer basket or steamer insert over a pot of boiling water. Cover and steam for 5-7 minutes, or until the vegetables are tender-crisp.
5. Serve:
   - Once the chicken is cooked through and the vegetables are steamed, remove them from the oven and steamer.
   - Arrange the baked chicken breasts on serving plates alongside the steamed vegetables.
   - Garnish with chopped fresh parsley and serve with lemon wedges on the side for squeezing over the chicken and vegetables, if desired.
6. Enjoy:
   - Serve the baked chicken breasts with steamed vegetables hot as a nutritious and satisfying meal.
   - You can pair this dish with cooked grains like rice or quinoa for a more filling meal, or enjoy it as is for a lighter option.

Stir-Fried Noodles with Vegetables

Stir-Fried Noodles with Vegetables

Ingredients:
- 8 ounces (about 225g) of your favorite noodles (such as spaghetti, rice noodles, or egg noodles)
- 2 tablespoons sesame oil or vegetable oil
- 3 cloves garlic, minced
- 1 small onion, thinly sliced
- 2 cups mixed vegetables (such as bell peppers, broccoli, carrots, snap peas, mushrooms, and baby corn)
- 3 tablespoons soy sauce (or tamari for gluten-free)
- 1 tablespoon oyster sauce (optional)
- 1 tablespoon rice vinegar or lime juice
- 1 teaspoon brown sugar or honey
- Salt and pepper, to taste
- Optional garnishes: chopped green onions, sesame seeds, cilantro, sliced chili peppers

Instructions:

1. Cook Noodles:
   - Cook the noodles according to the package instructions until they are al dente. Drain and rinse them under cold water to stop the cooking process. Set aside.
2. Prepare Vegetables:
   - Wash and chop the vegetables into bite-sized pieces. Keep any harder vegetables (like carrots and broccoli) separate from quicker-cooking ones (like bell peppers and snap peas).
3. Stir-Fry:
   - Heat the sesame oil or vegetable oil in a large skillet or wok over medium-high heat.
   - Add the minced garlic and sliced onion to the skillet. Stir-fry for 1-2 minutes until fragrant and the onion starts to soften.
4. Add Vegetables:
   - Add the harder vegetables to the skillet first (such as carrots and broccoli). Stir-fry for 2-3 minutes until they begin to soften.
   - Add the remaining vegetables to the skillet and continue to stir-fry for an additional 2-3 minutes until all the vegetables are tender-crisp.
5. Sauce:
   - In a small bowl, mix together the soy sauce, oyster sauce (if using), rice vinegar or lime juice, brown sugar or honey, salt, and pepper.
   - Pour the sauce mixture over the stir-fried vegetables in the skillet. Stir well to coat the vegetables evenly.
6. Combine with Noodles:
   - Add the cooked noodles to the skillet with the stir-fried vegetables and sauce. Toss everything together gently using tongs or a spatula until the noodles are heated through and well coated with the sauce.
7. Serve:
   - Transfer the stir-fried noodles with vegetables to serving plates or bowls.
   - Garnish with chopped green onions, sesame seeds, cilantro, and sliced chili peppers, if desired.
   - Serve hot and enjoy your delicious homemade stir-fried noodles with vegetables!

Margherita Pizza

Margherita Pizza

Ingredients:
- 1 pizza dough ball (store-bought or homemade)
- 1/2 cup pizza sauce or marinara sauce
- 8 ounces fresh mozzarella cheese, sliced
- 2-3 ripe tomatoes, thinly sliced
- Fresh basil leaves
- Extra virgin olive oil
- Salt and pepper, to taste
- Cornmeal or flour, for dusting

Instructions:
1. Preheat Oven:
   - Preheat your oven to the highest temperature it can go, typically around 500°F (260°C) or higher. Place a pizza stone or upside-down baking sheet in the oven to preheat as well.
2. Prepare Pizza Dough:
   - On a lightly floured surface, roll out the pizza dough into a round shape, about 12 inches in diameter. You can adjust the size to your preference.
   - Transfer the rolled-out dough to a pizza peel or parchment paper dusted with cornmeal or flour to prevent sticking.
3. Add Sauce and Toppings:
   - Spread the pizza sauce evenly over the rolled-out dough, leaving a small border around the edges.
   - Arrange the sliced fresh mozzarella cheese evenly over the sauce.
   - Place the thinly sliced tomatoes on top of the cheese.
   - Tear fresh basil leaves and scatter them over the pizza.
4. Season and Drizzle:
   - Drizzle a little extra virgin olive oil over the assembled pizza.
   - Season with salt and pepper to taste.
5. Bake Pizza:
   - Carefully transfer the assembled pizza onto the preheated pizza stone or baking sheet in the oven.
   - Bake for 10-12 minutes, or until the crust is golden brown and the cheese is bubbly and melted.
6. Serve:
   - Once the Margherita pizza is done baking, remove it from the oven and let it cool for a minute or two.
   - Slice the pizza into wedges using a pizza cutter or sharp knife.
   - Serve hot and enjoy your homemade Margherita pizza!

Margherita pizza is best enjoyed fresh out of the oven, with its simple yet vibrant flavors of tomatoes, mozzarella, and basil. It's a timeless classic that's sure to impress your family and friends!

Lentil Soup

Lentil Soup

Ingredients:
- 1 cup dried lentils (any variety), rinsed and picked over
- 1 tablespoon olive oil
- 1 onion, diced
- 2 carrots, diced
- 2 celery stalks, diced
- 3 cloves garlic, minced
- 1 teaspoon ground cumin
- 1 teaspoon ground coriander
- 1/2 teaspoon smoked paprika (optional, for extra flavor)
- 6 cups vegetable or chicken broth
- 1 (14.5-ounce) can diced tomatoes, undrained
- Salt and pepper, to taste
- Fresh lemon juice, for serving (optional)
- Chopped fresh parsley or cilantro, for garnish (optional)

Instructions:
1. Cook Lentils:
   - In a large pot, heat the olive oil over medium heat. Add the diced onion, carrots, and celery. Cook, stirring occasionally, until the vegetables are softened, about 5-7 minutes.
   - Add the minced garlic, ground cumin, ground coriander, and smoked paprika (if using). Cook for another 1-2 minutes until fragrant.
2. Add Broth and Tomatoes:
   - Pour in the vegetable or chicken broth and add the rinsed lentils to the pot. Stir to combine.
   - Add the diced tomatoes with their juices. Stir well.
3. Simmer Soup:
   - Bring the soup to a boil, then reduce the heat to low. Cover the pot and let the soup simmer for about 20-25 minutes, or until the lentils are tender.
4. Season:
   - Once the lentils are cooked, season the soup with salt and pepper to taste. Adjust the seasoning as needed.
5. Serve:
   - Ladle the hot lentil soup into serving bowls.
   - Squeeze a little fresh lemon juice over each bowl of soup, if desired, for a bright and fresh flavor.
   - Garnish with chopped fresh parsley or cilantro for added freshness and color.
6. Enjoy:
   - Serve the lentil soup hot as a comforting and nutritious meal.
   - Pair it with crusty bread or a side salad for a complete and satisfying lunch or dinner.

Feel free to customize this lentil soup recipe by adding other vegetables or spices according to your taste preferences. It's a versatile dish that's both delicious and good for you!

Baked Salmon with Lemon and Dill

Baked Salmon with Lemon and Dill

Ingredients:
- 4 salmon fillets (about 6 ounces each), skin-on or skinless
- Salt and pepper, to taste
- 2 tablespoons olive oil
- 2 tablespoons fresh lemon juice
- Zest of 1 lemon
- 2 cloves garlic, minced
- 2 tablespoons chopped fresh dill
- Lemon slices, for garnish (optional)

Instructions:

1. Preheat Oven:
   - Preheat your oven to 400°F (200°C). Line a baking sheet with parchment paper or lightly grease it with olive oil.
2. Prepare Salmon:
   - Pat the salmon fillets dry with paper towels. Season both sides of the salmon with salt and pepper to taste.
   - Place the salmon fillets on the prepared baking sheet, leaving some space between each fillet.
3. Make Lemon-Dill Marinade:
   - In a small bowl, whisk together the olive oil, fresh lemon juice, lemon zest, minced garlic, and chopped fresh dill until well combined.
4. Marinate Salmon:
   - Pour the lemon-dill marinade over the salmon fillets, coating them evenly. Use a brush or spoon to spread the marinade over the salmon.
5. Bake Salmon:
   - Place the baking sheet in the preheated oven and bake the salmon for 12-15 minutes, or until the salmon is cooked through and flakes easily with a fork. Cooking time may vary depending on the thickness of the salmon fillets.
6. Garnish and Serve:
   - Once the salmon is done baking, remove it from the oven and let it rest for a minute or two.
   - Garnish the baked salmon with additional chopped fresh dill and lemon slices, if desired, for presentation.
   - Serve the baked salmon hot with your favorite side dishes, such as roasted vegetables, rice, or salad.

This baked salmon with lemon and dill is a flavorful and nutritious dish that's perfect for weeknight dinners or special occasions. The combination of citrusy lemon and aromatic dill complements the natural richness of the salmon beautifully. Enjoy!

BLT Sandwich (Bacon, Lettuce, Tomato)

BLT Sandwich (Bacon, Lettuce, Tomato)

Ingredients:
- 8 slices of thick-cut bacon
- 4 slices of bread (white, whole wheat, or your favorite bread)
- 4 leaves of crisp lettuce (such as iceberg or romaine)
- 2 ripe tomatoes, thinly sliced
- Mayonnaise
- Salt and pepper, to taste

Instructions:
1. Cook Bacon:
   - In a large skillet over medium heat, cook the bacon slices until they are crispy and golden brown, turning occasionally to ensure even cooking. This usually takes about 8-10 minutes. Once cooked, transfer the bacon slices to a plate lined with paper towels to drain excess grease.
2. Toast Bread (optional):
   - If desired, toast the bread slices until they are golden brown and crispy.
3. Assemble Sandwich:
   - Spread a thin layer of mayonnaise on one side of each bread slice.
   - Place a leaf of lettuce on top of the mayonnaise on two of the bread slices.
   - Arrange the tomato slices on top of the lettuce.
   - Season the tomatoes with a sprinkle of salt and pepper, to taste.
   - Place the cooked bacon slices on top of the tomatoes.
   - Top with the remaining bread slices, mayonnaise side down, to form sandwiches.
4. Cut and Serve:
   - Using a sharp knife, cut each sandwich in half diagonally to create two triangular halves.
   - Serve the BLT sandwiches immediately, while the bacon is still warm and crispy.
5. Enjoy:
   - Enjoy your classic BLT sandwiches as a satisfying and delicious meal, perfect for lunch or a light dinner.

Feel free to customize your BLT sandwich by adding extras like avocado slices, cheese, or a fried egg. You can also experiment with different types of bread and spreads to suit your taste preferences.

Veggie Omelette

Veggie Omelette

Ingredients:
- 3 large eggs
- 1/4 cup diced bell peppers (any color)
- 1/4 cup diced onions
- 1/4 cup diced tomatoes
- 1/4 cup chopped spinach or kale
- 1/4 cup shredded cheese (such as cheddar, mozzarella, or feta)
- Salt and pepper, to taste
- 1 tablespoon butter or cooking oil

Optional Additions:
- Sliced mushrooms
- Diced zucchini
- Chopped broccoli
- Sliced avocado
- Diced ham or cooked bacon
- Fresh herbs (such as parsley or chives)

Instructions:
1. **Prepare Ingredients:**
   - Wash and chop the vegetables as needed. You can use any combination of vegetables you like or have on hand.
2. **Cook Vegetables:**
   - Heat the butter or cooking oil in a non-stick skillet over medium heat. Add the diced bell peppers and onions to the skillet and cook for 2-3 minutes until they start to soften.
   - Add the diced tomatoes and chopped spinach or kale to the skillet. Cook for another 1-2 minutes until the vegetables are tender. Season with salt and pepper to taste.
3. **Whisk Eggs:**
   - In a mixing bowl, crack the eggs and whisk them together until well beaten. Season with a pinch of salt and pepper.
4. **Pour Eggs into Skillet:**
   - Pour the beaten eggs evenly over the cooked vegetables in the skillet. Use a spatula to gently stir the eggs and vegetables together, allowing the uncooked eggs to flow to the bottom of the pan.
5. **Add Cheese:**
   - Once the eggs start to set on the bottom and around the edges, sprinkle the shredded cheese evenly over the top of the omelette.
6. **Fold Omelette:**
   - Using a spatula, carefully lift one side of the omelette and fold it over the other side to form a half-moon shape. Press down gently with the spatula to seal the omelette.
7. **Cook Until Set:**
   - Let the omelette cook for another 1-2 minutes, or until the cheese is melted and the eggs are fully set. You can gently press down on the omelette with the spatula to ensure it's cooked through.
8. **Serve:**
   - Slide the cooked omelette onto a plate. You can garnish it with additional cheese, chopped herbs, or a sprinkle of black pepper if desired.
   - Serve hot and enjoy your delicious veggie omelette!

Feel free to customize your veggie omelette with your favorite vegetables and cheese. It's a versatile dish that's perfect for breakfast, brunch, or even a quick and healthy dinner.

Beef or Veggie Burgers

Beef or Veggie Burgers

Beef Burgers:
Ingredients:
- 1 pound ground beef (preferably 80/20 lean to fat ratio)
- 1/4 cup breadcrumbs
- 1 egg
- 1/4 cup diced onion
- 1 clove garlic, minced
- 1 teaspoon Worcestershire sauce
- Salt and pepper, to taste
- Burger buns
- Optional toppings: lettuce, tomato, onion, cheese, ketchup, mustard, mayonnaise, pickles

Instructions:
1. Prepare Ingredients: In a mixing bowl, combine the ground beef, breadcrumbs, egg, diced onion, minced garlic, Worcestershire sauce, salt, and pepper. Mix until well combined.
2. Form Patties: Divide the beef mixture into equal portions and shape them into patties, about 1/2 inch thick. Make an indentation in the center of each patty with your thumb to prevent them from puffing up during cooking.
3. Cook Patties: Heat a grill or skillet over medium-high heat. Cook the beef patties for about 4-5 minutes on each side, or until they reach your desired level of doneness. Make sure to cook them to an internal temperature of at least 160°F (71°C).
4. Assemble Burgers: Toast the burger buns lightly. Place a cooked beef patty on the bottom half of each bun. Add your desired toppings, such as lettuce, tomato, onion, cheese, ketchup, mustard, and mayonnaise. Top with the other half of the bun.
5. Serve: Serve the beef burgers immediately while they're hot and enjoy!

Veggie Burgers:
Ingredients:
- 1 can (15 ounces) black beans, drained and rinsed
- 1/2 cup cooked quinoa or brown rice
- 1/4 cup finely chopped onion
- 1 clove garlic, minced
- 1 teaspoon ground cumin
- 1 teaspoon chili powder
- Salt and pepper, to taste
- 1/4 cup breadcrumbs
- 1 egg (or flax egg for vegan option)
- Burger buns
- Optional toppings: lettuce, tomato, onion, avocado, cheese, ketchup, mustard, mayonnaise

Instructions:
1. Prepare Ingredients: In a mixing bowl, mash the black beans with a fork until they form a chunky paste. Add the cooked quinoa or brown rice, chopped onion, minced garlic, ground cumin, chili powder, salt, and pepper. Mix until well combined.
2. Add Binding Agents: Stir in the breadcrumbs and egg (or flax egg) until the mixture holds together. If the mixture is too dry, you can add a little more breadcrumbs or a splash of water.
3. Form Patties: Divide the veggie mixture into equal portions and shape them into patties, about 1/2 inch thick.
4. Cook Patties: Heat a grill or skillet over medium heat. Cook the veggie patties for about 4-5 minutes on each side, or until they are heated through and lightly browned.
5. Assemble Burgers: Toast the burger buns lightly. Place a cooked veggie patty on the bottom half of each bun. Add your desired toppings, such as lettuce, tomato, onion, avocado, cheese, ketchup, mustard, and mayonnaise. Top with the other half of the bun.

Chicken Caesar Salad

Chicken Caesar Salad

Ingredients:
For the Salad:
- 2 boneless, skinless chicken breasts
- Salt and pepper, to taste
- 1 tablespoon olive oil
- 1 head of romaine lettuce, washed and chopped
- 1 cup cherry tomatoes, halved
- 1/2 cup grated Parmesan cheese
- 1 cup croutons (store-bought or homemade)
- Optional: Anchovies, for garnish

For the Caesar Dressing:
- 1/2 cup mayonnaise
- 2 tablespoons grated Parmesan cheese
- 2 tablespoons lemon juice
- 1 tablespoon Dijon mustard
- 1 clove garlic, minced
- 1 teaspoon Worcestershire sauce
- Salt and pepper, to taste

Instructions:
1. Grill Chicken:
   - Season the chicken breasts with salt and pepper on both sides.
   - Heat the olive oil in a grill pan or skillet over medium-high heat. Add the chicken breasts and cook for 6-8 minutes on each side, or until they are cooked through and no longer pink in the center. Remove from heat and let them rest for a few minutes before slicing.
2. Prepare Caesar Dressing:
   - In a small bowl, whisk together the mayonnaise, grated Parmesan cheese, lemon juice, Dijon mustard, minced garlic, Worcestershire sauce, salt, and pepper until smooth and well combined. Adjust the seasoning to taste.
3. Assemble Salad:
   - In a large mixing bowl, toss the chopped romaine lettuce with the cherry tomatoes, grated Parmesan cheese, and croutons.
   - Slice the grilled chicken breasts into thin strips and add them to the salad.
4. Add Dressing:
   - Pour the prepared Caesar dressing over the salad and toss until the ingredients are evenly coated with the dressing.
5. Garnish and Serve:
   - Garnish the salad with anchovies, if desired, for an authentic Caesar salad experience.
   - Divide the salad among serving plates or bowls.
   - Serve immediately as a main course or side dish.

This Chicken Caesar salad is perfect for a light and satisfying meal any day of the week. It's packed with flavor and textures that will leave you feeling satisfied and refreshed. Enjoy!

Chili Con Carne

Chili Con Carne

Ingredients:
- 1 tablespoon olive oil
- 1 large onion, chopped
- 3 cloves garlic, minced
- 1 pound ground beef
- 1 bell pepper, diced
- 1 can (14.5 ounces) diced tomatoes
- 1 can (15 ounces) kidney beans, drained and rinsed
- 1 can (15 ounces) black beans, drained and rinsed
- 2 tablespoons tomato paste
- 1 cup beef broth or water
- 2 tablespoons chili powder
- 1 teaspoon ground cumin
- 1 teaspoon paprika
- 1/2 teaspoon dried oregano
- Salt and pepper, to taste
- Optional toppings: shredded cheese, sour cream, chopped green onions, cilantro, avocado slices

Instructions:
1. Cook Aromatics: Heat the olive oil in a large pot or Dutch oven over medium heat. Add the chopped onion and minced garlic, and cook for 2-3 minutes until softened and fragrant.
2. Brown Ground Beef: Add the ground beef to the pot, breaking it up with a spoon. Cook, stirring occasionally, until the beef is browned and cooked through.
3. Add Bell Pepper and Spices: Stir in the diced bell pepper, chili powder, ground cumin, paprika, dried oregano, salt, and pepper. Cook for another 2-3 minutes to allow the spices to toast and become fragrant.
4. Add Tomatoes and Beans: Pour in the diced tomatoes (with their juices), drained and rinsed kidney beans, and drained and rinsed black beans. Stir in the tomato paste to thicken the chili.
5. Simmer: Pour in the beef broth or water to loosen the chili, if needed. Bring the chili to a simmer, then reduce the heat to low. Cover and let the chili simmer for at least 30 minutes to allow the flavors to meld together. Stir occasionally.
6. Adjust Seasoning: Taste the chili and adjust the seasoning with more salt, pepper, or spices if desired. If the chili is too thick, you can add more beef broth or water to reach your desired consistency.
7. Serve: Ladle the chili con carne into bowls and garnish with your favorite toppings, such as shredded cheese, sour cream, chopped green onions, cilantro, or avocado slices.
8. Enjoy: Serve the chili con carne hot and enjoy the hearty and comforting flavors!

This chili con carne recipe is perfect for feeding a crowd or for cozying up on a cold day. It's packed with protein and flavor, making it a satisfying meal on its own or served with cornbread, rice, or tortilla chips.

Pesto Pasta

Pesto Pasta

AIngredients:
For the Pesto Sauce:
- 2 cups fresh basil leaves, packed
- 1/2 cup grated Parmesan cheese
- 1/2 cup pine nuts or walnuts
- 3 cloves garlic, peeled
- 1/2 cup extra virgin olive oil
- Salt and pepper, to taste

For the Pasta:
- 12 ounces (340g) pasta (spaghetti, linguine, or your favorite pasta shape)
- Salt, for boiling water
- Optional: Cherry tomatoes, halved, for garnish
- Optional: Grated Parmesan cheese, for serving

Instructions:
1. Make Pesto Sauce:
   - In a food processor, combine the fresh basil leaves, grated Parmesan cheese, pine nuts or walnuts, and peeled garlic cloves. Pulse until the ingredients are finely chopped.
   - With the food processor running, gradually drizzle in the extra virgin olive oil until the mixture forms a smooth paste. Scrape down the sides of the food processor as needed.
   - Season the pesto sauce with salt and pepper to taste. Adjust the seasoning as needed.
2. Cook Pasta:
   - Bring a large pot of salted water to a boil. Add the pasta and cook according to the package instructions until it is al dente. Reserve about 1/2 cup of the pasta cooking water before draining the pasta.
3. Combine Pasta and Pesto:
   - In a large mixing bowl, toss the cooked pasta with the pesto sauce until the pasta is evenly coated. If the pasta seems dry, you can add a splash of the reserved pasta cooking water to loosen the sauce.
4. Garnish and Serve:
   - Optional: Garnish the pesto pasta with halved cherry tomatoes for extra freshness and color.
   - Serve the pesto pasta hot, topped with grated Parmesan cheese if desired.
   - You can also serve the pesto pasta as a side dish or main course, accompanied by a simple green salad or crusty bread.
5. Enjoy:
   - Enjoy your homemade pesto pasta, savoring the vibrant flavors of fresh basil, Parmesan cheese, and garlic in every bite!

This pesto pasta recipe is quick and easy to make, perfect for a weeknight dinner or a casual gathering with friends and family. Feel free to customize it by adding cooked chicken, shrimp, or roasted vegetables for extra protein and texture.

Grilled Chicken with Roasted Vegetables

Grilled Chicken with Roasted Vegetables

Ingredients:
For the Grilled Chicken:
- 4 boneless, skinless chicken breasts
- 2 tablespoons olive oil
- 2 cloves garlic, minced
- 1 teaspoon dried oregano
- 1 teaspoon dried thyme
- Salt and pepper, to taste

For the Roasted Vegetables:
- 2 bell peppers, seeded and sliced
- 1 red onion, peeled and sliced
- 2 zucchini, sliced
- 1 eggplant, sliced
- 2 tablespoons olive oil
- 2 cloves garlic, minced
- 1 teaspoon dried Italian herbs (such as basil, oregano, and thyme)
- Salt and pepper, to taste

Instructions:

1. Marinate Chicken:
   - In a mixing bowl, combine the olive oil, minced garlic, dried oregano, dried thyme, salt, and pepper. Stir to create a marinade.
   - Add the chicken breasts to the marinade and toss to coat them evenly. Cover the bowl and let the chicken marinate in the refrigerator for at least 30 minutes, or up to 4 hours.
2. Preheat Grill:
   - Preheat your grill to medium-high heat.
3. Prepare Vegetables:
   - In a large mixing bowl, combine the sliced bell peppers, red onion, zucchini, eggplant, olive oil, minced garlic, dried Italian herbs, salt, and pepper. Toss until the vegetables are evenly coated with the seasoning.
4. Grill Chicken:
   - Remove the marinated chicken breasts from the refrigerator and let them come to room temperature for about 10 minutes.
   - Place the chicken breasts on the preheated grill and cook for 6-8 minutes per side, or until they are cooked through and no longer pink in the center. Cooking time may vary depending on the thickness of the chicken breasts. Use a meat thermometer to ensure the internal temperature reaches 165°F (75°C).
5. Roast Vegetables:
   - While the chicken is grilling, spread the seasoned vegetables in a single layer on a large baking sheet lined with parchment paper or aluminum foil.
   - Roast the vegetables in the preheated oven at 400°F (200°C) for 20-25 minutes, or until they are tender and lightly browned, stirring halfway through the cooking time.
6. Serve:
   - Once the chicken is cooked through and the vegetables are roasted, remove them from the grill and oven.
   - Serve the grilled chicken with the roasted vegetables on the side.
   - Optionally, garnish with fresh herbs like parsley or basil for extra flavor and presentation.
7. Enjoy:
   - Enjoy your delicious grilled chicken with roasted vegetables as a nutritious and satisfying meal!

This grilled chicken with roasted vegetables recipe is versatile and can be customized with your favorite seasonings and vegetables. It's perfect for a healthy weeknight dinner or a weekend barbecue with friends and family.

Ratatouille

Ratatouille

Ingredients:
- 1 large eggplant, diced into 1-inch cubes
- 2 medium zucchini, diced into 1-inch cubes
- 1 large yellow onion, diced
- 1 red bell pepper, diced
- 1 yellow bell pepper, diced
- 3 cloves garlic, minced
- 4 ripe tomatoes, diced
- 2 tablespoons tomato paste
- 2 tablespoons olive oil
- 1 teaspoon dried thyme
- 1 teaspoon dried oregano
- 1 teaspoon dried basil
- Salt and pepper, to taste
- Fresh basil leaves, chopped, for garnish

Instructions:

1. Prepare Vegetables:
   - Start by preparing all the vegetables. Dice the eggplant, zucchini, onion, red bell pepper, yellow bell pepper, and tomatoes into 1-inch cubes. Mince the garlic cloves.
2. Sauté Vegetables:
   - Heat the olive oil in a large skillet or Dutch oven over medium heat. Add the diced onion and minced garlic to the skillet and cook for 2-3 minutes until softened and fragrant.
   - Add the diced eggplant, zucchini, red bell pepper, and yellow bell pepper to the skillet. Cook, stirring occasionally, for 5-7 minutes until the vegetables start to soften.
3. Add Tomatoes and Seasonings:
   - Stir in the diced tomatoes and tomato paste to the skillet, mixing well to combine with the vegetables.
   - Add the dried thyme, dried oregano, dried basil, salt, and pepper to the skillet. Stir to distribute the seasonings evenly.
4. Simmer:
   - Reduce the heat to low and let the ratatouille simmer, uncovered, for 20-25 minutes, stirring occasionally, until the vegetables are tender and the flavors have melded together. If the mixture becomes too dry, you can add a splash of water or vegetable broth to loosen it up.
5. Adjust Seasoning:
   - Taste the ratatouille and adjust the seasoning with salt and pepper if needed. You can also add more herbs or garlic according to your taste preferences.
6. Serve:
   - Once the ratatouille is done cooking, remove it from the heat.
   - Serve the ratatouille hot, garnished with chopped fresh basil leaves for extra flavor and freshness.
7. Enjoy:
   - Enjoy your homemade ratatouille as a delicious side dish or main course, served with crusty bread, rice, or quinoa.

Ratatouille is a versatile dish that can be enjoyed hot, cold, or at room temperature. It's a celebration of seasonal vegetables and Mediterranean flavors that's perfect for any occasion!

Teriyaki Chicken with Rice

Teriyaki Chicken with Rice

Ingredients:
For the Teriyaki Chicken:
- 4 boneless, skinless chicken breasts
- 1/2 cup soy sauce
- 1/4 cup mirin (Japanese sweet rice wine)
- 2 tablespoons honey or brown sugar
- 2 cloves garlic, minced
- 1 teaspoon grated ginger
- 2 tablespoons vegetable oil
- Sesame seeds, for garnish (optional)
- Sliced green onions, for garnish (optional)

For the Rice:
- 1 cup jasmine rice (or any type of rice you prefer)
- 2 cups water
- Pinch of salt

Instructions:
1. Marinate Chicken:
   - In a mixing bowl, combine the soy sauce, mirin, honey or brown sugar, minced garlic, and grated ginger to make the teriyaki sauce.
   - Place the chicken breasts in a shallow dish or resealable plastic bag. Pour half of the teriyaki sauce over the chicken, reserving the other half for later. Marinate the chicken in the refrigerator for at least 30 minutes, or up to 2 hours.
2. Cook Rice:
   - Rinse the jasmine rice under cold water until the water runs clear. This helps remove excess starch and prevents the rice from becoming too sticky.
   - In a medium saucepan, combine the rinsed rice, water, and a pinch of salt. Bring to a boil over high heat.
   - Once boiling, reduce the heat to low, cover the saucepan with a tight-fitting lid, and simmer for 15-20 minutes, or until the rice is cooked and all the water is absorbed. Remove from heat and let it sit, covered, for 5 minutes before fluffing with a fork.
3. Cook Chicken:
   - Heat the vegetable oil in a large skillet or grill pan over medium-high heat. Remove the chicken breasts from the marinade and discard the excess marinade.
   - Add the chicken breasts to the hot skillet and cook for 6-8 minutes on each side, or until they are cooked through and no longer pink in the center. Cooking time may vary depending on the thickness of the chicken breasts.
   - While the chicken is cooking, you can brush it with some of the reserved teriyaki sauce for extra flavor.
4. Serve:
   - Once the chicken is cooked through, remove it from the skillet and let it rest for a few minutes before slicing it into strips.
   - Serve the sliced teriyaki chicken over cooked rice, drizzled with the remaining teriyaki sauce.
   - Garnish with sesame seeds and sliced green onions, if desired, for extra flavor and presentation.
5. Enjoy:

Greek Salad with Grilled Chicken

Greek Salad with Grilled Chicken

Ingredients:

For the Grilled Chicken:
- 4 boneless, skinless chicken breasts
- 2 tablespoons olive oil
- 2 cloves garlic, minced
- 1 teaspoon dried oregano
- Salt and pepper, to taste

For the Greek Salad:
- 1 large cucumber, diced
- 4 medium tomatoes, diced
- 1 red onion, thinly sliced
- 1 cup Kalamata olives, pitted
- 1 cup crumbled feta cheese
- 1/4 cup chopped fresh parsley
- 1/4 cup extra virgin olive oil
- 2 tablespoons red wine vinegar
- 1 teaspoon dried oregano
- Salt and pepper, to taste
- Optional: Sliced bell peppers, sliced pepperoncini peppers, sliced avocado

Instructions:

1. Marinate Chicken:
   - In a mixing bowl, combine the olive oil, minced garlic, dried oregano, salt, and pepper to make the marinade.
   - Place the chicken breasts in a shallow dish or resealable plastic bag. Pour the marinade over the chicken, making sure it's evenly coated. Marinate the chicken in the refrigerator for at least 30 minutes, or up to 2 hours.

2. Grill Chicken:
   - Preheat your grill to medium-high heat. Remove the chicken breasts from the marinade and discard the excess marinade.
   - Grill the chicken breasts for 6-8 minutes on each side, or until they are cooked through and no longer pink in the center. Cooking time may vary depending on the thickness of the chicken breasts. Use a meat thermometer to ensure the internal temperature reaches 165°F (75°C).

3. Prepare Greek Salad:
   - In a large mixing bowl, combine the diced cucumber, diced tomatoes, thinly sliced red onion, pitted Kalamata olives, crumbled feta cheese, and chopped fresh parsley.
   - In a small bowl, whisk together the extra virgin olive oil, red wine vinegar, dried oregano, salt, and pepper to make the dressing.

4. Assemble Salad:
   - Pour the dressing over the Greek salad ingredients in the mixing bowl. Toss gently to coat the vegetables and cheese with the dressing.

5. Serve:
   - Divide the Greek salad among serving plates or bowls.
   - Slice the grilled chicken breasts into strips and arrange them on top of the Greek salad.
   - Optionally, garnish the salad with additional chopped parsley and a sprinkle of crumbled feta cheese.

6. Enjoy:
   - Serve the Greek salad with grilled chicken immediately, and enjoy the vibrant flavors of the Mediterranean!

Tuna Salad Sandwich

Tuna Salad Sandwich

Ingredients:
- 1 can (5 oz) tuna, drained
- 2 tablespoons mayonnaise
- 1 tablespoon chopped celery
- 1 tablespoon chopped red onion
- 1 teaspoon Dijon mustard (optional)
- Salt and pepper to taste
- Squeeze of lemon juice (optional)
- 2 slices bread
- Lettuce leaves (optional)
- Tomato slices (optional)

Instructions:
1. In a bowl, mix together the tuna, mayonnaise, chopped celery, chopped red onion, Dijon mustard (if using), salt, pepper, and lemon juice (if using).
2. Spread the tuna salad mixture evenly onto one slice of bread.
3. If desired, add lettuce leaves and tomato slices on top of the tuna salad.
4. Top with the other slice of bread to make a sandwich.
5. Cut the sandwich in half diagonally and serve.

Feel free to customize the recipe to your taste preferences! You can add ingredients like diced pickles, capers, or herbs for extra flavor. Enjoy your tuna salad sandwich!

Spinach and Feta Stuffed Chicken Breast

Spinach and Feta Stuffed Chicken Breast

Ingredients:
- 2 boneless, skinless chicken breasts
- 2 cups fresh spinach leaves, washed and chopped
- 1/2 cup crumbled feta cheese
- 2 cloves garlic, minced
- 1 tablespoon olive oil
- Salt and pepper to taste
- Toothpicks or kitchen twine

Instructions:
1. Preheat your oven to 375°F (190°C).
2. In a skillet, heat the olive oil over medium heat. Add the minced garlic and cook for about 1 minute until fragrant.
3. Add the chopped spinach to the skillet and sauté until wilted, about 2-3 minutes. Season with salt and pepper to taste. Remove from heat and let cool slightly.
4. While the spinach is cooling, use a sharp knife to cut a pocket into the side of each chicken breast, being careful not to cut all the way through.
5. Stuff each chicken breast with equal amounts of the sautéed spinach and crumbled feta cheese. Secure the openings with toothpicks or tie with kitchen twine to keep the filling inside.
6. Season the outside of the chicken breasts with salt and pepper.
7. Heat a bit more olive oil in an oven-safe skillet over medium-high heat. Once hot, add the stuffed chicken breasts to the skillet and cook for about 3-4 minutes per side, until golden brown.
8. Transfer the skillet to the preheated oven and bake for an additional 15-20 minutes, or until the chicken is cooked through and reaches an internal temperature of 165°F (74°C).
9. Once cooked, remove the chicken from the oven and let it rest for a few minutes before serving.
10. Serve the spinach and feta stuffed chicken breasts hot, garnished with fresh herbs if desired. Enjoy!

Shrimp Stir-Fry

Shrimp Stir-Fry

Ingredients:
- 1 lb (450g) large shrimp, peeled and deveined
- 2 tablespoons soy sauce
- 1 tablespoon oyster sauce
- 1 tablespoon hoisin sauce
- 1 tablespoon sesame oil
- 2 cloves garlic, minced
- 1 teaspoon grated ginger
- 1 onion, sliced
- 1 bell pepper, sliced
- 1 cup broccoli florets
- 1 carrot, julienned
- 2 green onions, chopped (for garnish)
- Cooked rice or noodles, for serving

Instructions:
1. In a small bowl, mix together the soy sauce, oyster sauce, hoisin sauce, and sesame oil. Set aside.
2. Heat a bit of oil in a large skillet or wok over medium-high heat. Add the minced garlic and grated ginger, and stir-fry for about 30 seconds until fragrant.
3. Add the sliced onion to the skillet and stir-fry for 1-2 minutes until it begins to soften.
4. Add the bell pepper, broccoli florets, and julienned carrot to the skillet. Stir-fry for another 2-3 minutes until the vegetables are crisp-tender.
5. Push the vegetables to one side of the skillet and add the shrimp to the other side. Cook the shrimp for 2-3 minutes, stirring occasionally, until they turn pink and opaque.
6. Pour the sauce mixture over the shrimp and vegetables in the skillet. Stir everything together until the shrimp and vegetables are evenly coated in the sauce.
7. Cook for another minute or two until the sauce thickens slightly.
8. Remove the skillet from the heat and sprinkle chopped green onions on top for garnish.
9. Serve the shrimp stir-fry hot over cooked rice or noodles.

Feel free to customize this recipe by adding your favorite vegetables or adjusting the sauce to your taste preferences. Enjoy your delicious shrimp stir-fry!

Vegetable Curry

Vegetable Curry

Ingredients:
- 2 tablespoons vegetable oil
- 1 onion, diced
- 2 cloves garlic, minced
- 1 tablespoon grated ginger
- 2 tablespoons curry powder
- 1 teaspoon ground turmeric
- 1 teaspoon ground cumin
- 1 teaspoon ground coriander
- 1/2 teaspoon ground cinnamon
- 1 can (14 oz) coconut milk
- 2 cups vegetable broth
- 2 potatoes, peeled and diced
- 2 carrots, peeled and sliced
- 1 bell pepper, diced
- 1 cup cauliflower florets
- 1 cup green beans, trimmed and cut into bite-sized pieces
- Salt and pepper to taste
- Fresh cilantro leaves, chopped (for garnish)
- Cooked rice or naan bread, for serving

Instructions:
1. Heat the vegetable oil in a large pot or Dutch oven over medium heat. Add the diced onion and cook until softened, about 3-4 minutes.
2. Add the minced garlic and grated ginger to the pot, and cook for another minute until fragrant.
3. Stir in the curry powder, ground turmeric, ground cumin, ground coriander, and ground cinnamon. Cook for 1-2 minutes, stirring constantly, to toast the spices.
4. Pour in the coconut milk and vegetable broth, and stir until well combined.
5. Add the diced potatoes, sliced carrots, diced bell pepper, cauliflower florets, and green beans to the pot. Stir to combine.
6. Bring the curry to a simmer, then reduce the heat to low and cover the pot. Let the curry cook for about 20-25 minutes, stirring occasionally, until the vegetables are tender.
7. Season the curry with salt and pepper to taste.
8. Serve the vegetable curry hot, garnished with chopped cilantro leaves. Enjoy with cooked rice or naan bread on the side.

Feel free to customize this vegetable curry by adding your favorite vegetables or adjusting the spices to suit your taste preferences. Enjoy your comforting and flavorful meal!

Bruschetta with Tomato and Basil

Bruschetta with Tomato and Basil

Ingredients:
- 4-6 slices of crusty bread (like baguette or Italian bread)
- 2-3 ripe tomatoes, diced
- 1-2 cloves of garlic, minced
- 5-6 fresh basil leaves, thinly sliced (chiffonade)
- 2 tablespoons extra virgin olive oil
- 1 teaspoon balsamic vinegar (optional)
- Salt and pepper to taste

Instructions:
1. Preheat your oven to 400°F (200°C). Arrange the slices of bread on a baking sheet and drizzle them lightly with olive oil.
2. Toast the bread in the preheated oven for about 5-7 minutes, or until it's lightly golden and crispy. Keep an eye on it to prevent burning.
3. While the bread is toasting, prepare the tomato topping. In a bowl, combine the diced tomatoes, minced garlic, thinly sliced basil leaves, extra virgin olive oil, and balsamic vinegar (if using). Season with salt and pepper to taste.
4. Once the bread is toasted, remove it from the oven and let it cool slightly.
5. Spoon the tomato mixture generously onto each slice of toasted bread, allowing the juices to soak into the bread.
6. Serve the bruschetta immediately as an appetizer or snack.

Beef Stew

Beef Stew

Ingredients:
- 2 lbs (about 900g) beef stew meat, cut into bite-sized pieces
- 2 tablespoons all-purpose flour
- Salt and pepper to taste
- 2 tablespoons vegetable oil or olive oil
- 1 onion, diced
- 2-3 cloves garlic, minced
- 4 cups beef broth
- 1 cup red wine (optional)
- 2 bay leaves
- 1 teaspoon dried thyme
- 1 teaspoon dried rosemary
- 4 carrots, peeled and sliced
- 3 potatoes, peeled and diced
- 2 stalks celery, sliced
- 1 cup frozen peas (optional)
- Chopped fresh parsley (for garnish)

Instructions:
1. In a large bowl, season the beef stew meat with salt and pepper. Add the flour and toss to coat the meat evenly.
2. Heat the vegetable oil or olive oil in a large Dutch oven or heavy-bottomed pot over medium-high heat. Add the coated beef stew meat in batches and brown on all sides. Remove the browned meat from the pot and set aside.
3. In the same pot, add the diced onion and minced garlic. Cook, stirring occasionally, until the onions are softened and translucent, about 3-4 minutes.
4. Return the browned beef stew meat to the pot. Pour in the beef broth and red wine (if using), scraping up any browned bits from the bottom of the pot.
5. Add the bay leaves, dried thyme, and dried rosemary to the pot. Stir to combine.
6. Bring the stew to a simmer, then reduce the heat to low. Cover the pot and let the stew simmer gently for about 1 1/2 to 2 hours, or until the beef is tender.
7. Once the beef is tender, add the sliced carrots, diced potatoes, and sliced celery to the pot. Cover and continue to simmer for another 30 minutes, or until the vegetables are tender.
8. If using frozen peas, add them to the pot during the last 5 minutes of cooking.
9. Taste the stew and adjust the seasoning with salt and pepper if needed.
10. Serve the beef stew hot, garnished with chopped fresh parsley.

Beef stew is delicious served with crusty bread or over cooked rice or mashed potatoes. Enjoy this comforting and hearty dish!

Baked Ziti

Baked Ziti

Ingredients:
- 1 lb (450g) ziti pasta
- 1 tablespoon olive oil
- 1 onion, chopped
- 2 cloves garlic, minced
- 1 lb (450g) ground beef or Italian sausage (optional)
- 1 jar (24 oz) marinara sauce
- 1 cup ricotta cheese
- 1 cup shredded mozzarella cheese
- 1/2 cup grated Parmesan cheese
- 1/4 cup chopped fresh basil or parsley (optional)
- Salt and pepper to taste

Instructions:
1. Preheat your oven to 375°F (190°C). Grease a 9x13-inch baking dish with non-stick cooking spray or olive oil.
2. Cook the ziti pasta according to the package instructions until al dente. Drain the pasta and set aside.
3. In a large skillet, heat the olive oil over medium heat. Add the chopped onion and minced garlic, and cook until softened, about 3-4 minutes.
4. If using, add the ground beef or Italian sausage to the skillet. Cook, breaking up the meat with a spoon, until browned and cooked through. Drain off any excess fat.
5. Pour the marinara sauce into the skillet with the cooked meat mixture. Stir to combine, then let it simmer for a few minutes to heat through.
6. In a large mixing bowl, combine the cooked ziti pasta with the meat sauce mixture. Add the ricotta cheese, shredded mozzarella cheese, grated Parmesan cheese, chopped fresh basil or parsley (if using), and salt and pepper to taste. Mix everything together until well combined.
7. Transfer the ziti mixture to the prepared baking dish, spreading it out evenly.
8. Cover the baking dish with aluminum foil and bake in the preheated oven for 25 minutes.
9. After 25 minutes, remove the foil from the baking dish and continue to bake for an additional 10-15 minutes, or until the top is golden and bubbly.
10. Once baked, remove the ziti from the oven and let it cool for a few minutes before serving.
11. Serve the baked ziti hot, garnished with additional chopped fresh basil or parsley if desired.

Baked ziti pairs well with a side salad and garlic bread for a complete meal. Enjoy this delicious and comforting dish!

Lemon Garlic Shrimp Pasta

Lemon Garlic Shrimp Pasta

Ingredients:
- 8 oz (225g) linguine or spaghetti
- 1 lb (450g) large shrimp, peeled and deveined
- Salt and pepper to taste
- 2 tablespoons olive oil
- 4 cloves garlic, minced
- Zest of 1 lemon
- Juice of 1 lemon
- 1/2 cup chicken broth or white wine
- 2 tablespoons unsalted butter
- 2 tablespoons chopped fresh parsley
- Grated Parmesan cheese (optional), for serving

Instructions:
1. Cook the linguine or spaghetti according to the package instructions until al dente. Drain the pasta and set aside.
2. While the pasta is cooking, season the shrimp with salt and pepper to taste.
3. Heat the olive oil in a large skillet over medium-high heat. Add the seasoned shrimp to the skillet and cook for 2-3 minutes on each side, until pink and opaque. Remove the shrimp from the skillet and set aside.
4. In the same skillet, add the minced garlic and cook for about 1 minute until fragrant.
5. Add the lemon zest, lemon juice, and chicken broth or white wine to the skillet. Bring the mixture to a simmer and let it cook for 2-3 minutes, allowing the flavors to meld together.
6. Reduce the heat to low and stir in the unsalted butter until melted and the sauce is slightly thickened.
7. Return the cooked shrimp to the skillet and toss to coat them in the lemon garlic sauce.
8. Add the cooked linguine or spaghetti to the skillet and toss everything together until the pasta is evenly coated in the sauce.
9. Stir in the chopped fresh parsley.
10. Taste and adjust the seasoning with salt and pepper if needed.
11. Serve the lemon garlic shrimp pasta hot, garnished with grated Parmesan cheese if desired.

This lemon garlic shrimp pasta is delicious served with a side of garlic bread and a simple salad. Enjoy!

Chicken Fajitas

Chicken Fajitas

Ingredients:
- 1 lb (450g) boneless, skinless chicken breasts, thinly sliced
- 2 tablespoons olive oil
- 1 onion, sliced
- 1 bell pepper (any color), sliced
- 2 cloves garlic, minced
- 1 tablespoon chili powder
- 1 teaspoon ground cumin
- 1/2 teaspoon paprika
- 1/2 teaspoon garlic powder
- 1/2 teaspoon onion powder
- Salt and pepper to taste
- Juice of 1 lime
- Tortillas, for serving
- Optional toppings: salsa, sour cream, guacamole, shredded cheese, chopped cilantro, sliced jalapeños

Instructions:
1. In a small bowl, mix together the chili powder, ground cumin, paprika, garlic powder, onion powder, salt, and pepper to make the fajita seasoning.
2. Heat 1 tablespoon of olive oil in a large skillet over medium-high heat. Add the sliced chicken breasts to the skillet and sprinkle half of the fajita seasoning over the chicken. Cook, stirring occasionally, until the chicken is cooked through and no longer pink, about 5-6 minutes. Remove the cooked chicken from the skillet and set aside.
3. In the same skillet, add the remaining 1 tablespoon of olive oil. Add the sliced onion and bell pepper to the skillet and sprinkle the remaining fajita seasoning over the vegetables. Cook, stirring occasionally, until the vegetables are tender-crisp, about 4-5 minutes.
4. Add the minced garlic to the skillet with the vegetables and cook for an additional minute until fragrant.
5. Return the cooked chicken to the skillet with the vegetables. Squeeze the juice of 1 lime over the chicken and vegetables. Stir everything together and cook for another minute to heat through.
6. Remove the skillet from the heat.
7. Warm the tortillas in a separate skillet or in the microwave according to package instructions.
8. Serve the chicken fajita mixture hot, spooned into warm tortillas. Top with your favorite toppings such as salsa, sour cream, guacamole, shredded cheese, chopped cilantro, and sliced jalapeños.
9. Roll up the tortillas and enjoy your delicious chicken fajitas!

These chicken fajitas are versatile, so feel free to customize them with additional toppings or add-ins according to your preferences. Enjoy!

Roasted Vegetable Quinoa Bowl

Roasted Vegetable Quinoa Bowl

Ingredients:
- 1 cup quinoa, rinsed
- 2 cups water or vegetable broth
- Assorted vegetables (e.g., bell peppers, zucchini, carrots, broccoli, cauliflower, cherry tomatoes)
- Olive oil
- Salt and pepper to taste
- Optional toppings: avocado slices, fresh herbs, toasted nuts or seeds

For the dressing:
- 1/4 cup olive oil
- 2 tablespoons balsamic vinegar or lemon juice
- 1 garlic clove, minced
- 1 teaspoon Dijon mustard
- Salt and pepper to taste

Instructions:
1. Preheat your oven to 400°F (200°C).
2. Chop your vegetables into bite-sized pieces and spread them out on a baking sheet. Drizzle with olive oil and season with salt and pepper. Toss to coat evenly.
3. Roast the vegetables in the preheated oven for 20-25 minutes or until they are tender and slightly caramelized, stirring halfway through.
4. While the vegetables are roasting, prepare the quinoa. In a medium saucepan, combine the rinsed quinoa and water or vegetable broth. Bring to a boil, then reduce the heat to low, cover, and simmer for about 15 minutes or until the quinoa is cooked and the liquid is absorbed. Remove from heat and let it sit, covered, for 5 minutes. Fluff with a fork.
5. In a small bowl, whisk together all the ingredients for the dressing until well combined.
6. To assemble the bowls, divide the cooked quinoa among serving bowls. Top with the roasted vegetables and any additional toppings you like.
7. Drizzle the dressing over the bowls just before serving, and enjoy!

Feel free to customize this recipe based on your preferences and the vegetables you have on hand. It's a versatile dish that's perfect for meal prep or a quick and healthy weeknight dinner.

Pan-Seared Steak with Mashed Potatoes

Pan-Seared Steak with Mashed Potatoes

Ingredients:
- 2 boneless steaks (such as ribeye, strip loin, or filet mignon), about 1 inch thick
- Salt and pepper to taste
- 2 tablespoons olive oil or butter
- 4 large potatoes, peeled and quartered
- 1/2 cup milk or cream
- 2 tablespoons butter
- Salt and pepper to taste
- Optional: minced garlic, chopped fresh herbs (such as parsley or chives)

Instructions:

For the Mashed Potatoes:
1. Place the quartered potatoes in a large pot and cover with cold water. Add a generous pinch of salt to the water.
2. Bring the water to a boil over high heat. Reduce the heat to medium-low and simmer the potatoes until they are fork-tender, about 15-20 minutes.
3. Once the potatoes are cooked, drain them in a colander and return them to the pot.
4. Add the milk or cream and butter to the pot with the potatoes. Use a potato masher or a fork to mash the potatoes until smooth and creamy. Season with salt and pepper to taste.
5. If desired, add minced garlic or chopped fresh herbs to the mashed potatoes for extra flavor. Keep warm until ready to serve.

For the Pan-Seared Steak:
1. Pat the steaks dry with paper towels and season them generously with salt and pepper on both sides.
2. Heat a large skillet over medium-high heat. Add the olive oil or butter to the skillet and swirl to coat the bottom.
3. Once the skillet is hot, carefully add the steaks. Cook undisturbed for 3-4 minutes on one side until a golden crust forms.
4. Flip the steaks and continue to cook for an additional 3-4 minutes for medium-rare doneness, or adjust the cooking time according to your desired level of doneness.
5. Remove the steaks from the skillet and let them rest on a cutting board for a few minutes before slicing.
6. Serve the pan-seared steaks with the mashed potatoes, and enjoy!

Feel free to customize this recipe by adding your favorite steak seasoning or serving the steak with a side of sautéed vegetables for a complete meal.

Stuffed Bell Peppers

Stuffed Bell Peppers

Ingredients:
- 4 large bell peppers (any color), halved and seeds removed
- 1 cup cooked rice (white or brown)
- 1 pound ground meat (beef, turkey, chicken, or vegetarian substitute)
- 1 onion, finely chopped
- 2 cloves garlic, minced
- 1 can (14.5 oz) diced tomatoes, drained
- 1 cup shredded cheese (such as cheddar or mozzarella)
- 1 teaspoon dried oregano
- 1 teaspoon dried basil
- Salt and pepper to taste
- Olive oil

Instructions:
1. Preheat your oven to 375°F (190°C).
2. Heat a large skillet over medium heat. Add a drizzle of olive oil, then add the chopped onion and minced garlic. Cook until softened and fragrant, about 3-4 minutes.
3. Add the ground meat to the skillet, breaking it up with a spoon. Cook until browned and cooked through, about 5-7 minutes. Drain any excess fat if necessary.
4. Stir in the cooked rice, diced tomatoes, dried oregano, dried basil, salt, and pepper. Cook for an additional 2-3 minutes until everything is well combined and heated through. Taste and adjust seasoning if needed.
5. Place the bell pepper halves in a baking dish, cut side up. Fill each pepper half with the meat and rice mixture, pressing down gently to pack it in.
6. Sprinkle shredded cheese over the top of each stuffed pepper.
7. Cover the baking dish with foil and bake in the preheated oven for 25-30 minutes, or until the peppers are tender and the cheese is melted and bubbly.
8. Remove the foil and bake for an additional 5 minutes to lightly brown the cheese, if desired.
9. Once done, remove from the oven and let the stuffed bell peppers cool for a few minutes before serving.
10. Serve the stuffed bell peppers hot, garnished with fresh herbs if desired, and enjoy!

Feel free to customize the filling by adding other ingredients such as black beans, corn, diced vegetables, or your favorite herbs and spices. It's a versatile dish that can easily be adapted to suit your taste preferences!

Chicken and Broccoli Stir-Fry

Chicken and Broccoli Stir-Fry

Ingredients:
- 1 lb (450g) boneless, skinless chicken breasts, thinly sliced
- 2 cups broccoli florets
- 1 bell pepper, thinly sliced (optional)
- 2 cloves garlic, minced
- 2 tablespoons soy sauce
- 1 tablespoon oyster sauce (optional)
- 1 tablespoon hoisin sauce (optional)
- 1 tablespoon cornstarch
- 1/4 cup chicken broth or water
- 2 tablespoons vegetable oil, divided
- Salt and pepper to taste
- Cooked rice or noodles for serving

Instructions:
1. In a small bowl, whisk together the soy sauce, oyster sauce, hoisin sauce (if using), cornstarch, and chicken broth until smooth. Set aside.
2. Heat 1 tablespoon of vegetable oil in a large skillet or wok over medium-high heat. Add the sliced chicken to the skillet and season with salt and pepper. Stir-fry for 5-6 minutes, or until the chicken is cooked through and no longer pink. Remove the chicken from the skillet and set aside.
3. In the same skillet, add the remaining tablespoon of vegetable oil. Add the minced garlic and stir-fry for about 30 seconds, or until fragrant.
4. Add the broccoli florets and bell pepper (if using) to the skillet. Stir-fry for 3-4 minutes, or until the vegetables are tender-crisp.
5. Return the cooked chicken to the skillet with the vegetables. Pour the sauce mixture over the chicken and vegetables, stirring constantly.
6. Continue to cook for another 2-3 minutes, or until the sauce has thickened and everything is heated through.
7. Taste and adjust seasoning if needed. If the sauce is too thick, you can add a splash of chicken broth or water to thin it out.
8. Once done, remove the skillet from the heat. Serve the chicken and broccoli stir-fry hot over cooked rice or noodles.
9. Garnish with sliced green onions or sesame seeds if desired, and enjoy!

Feel free to customize this recipe by adding other vegetables such as carrots, snap peas, or mushrooms. You can also adjust the level of sauce according to your preference by adding more or less of the soy sauce mixture.

Thai Peanut Noodles

Thai Peanut Noodles

Ingredients:
- 8 oz (225g) rice noodles or any other noodles of your choice
- 1/4 cup creamy peanut butter
- 3 tablespoons soy sauce
- 2 tablespoons rice vinegar
- 1 tablespoon sesame oil
- 1 tablespoon honey or maple syrup
- 1 tablespoon freshly squeezed lime juice
- 2 cloves garlic, minced
- 1 teaspoon grated fresh ginger
- 1/4 teaspoon red pepper flakes (adjust to taste)
- 1/4 cup water (more as needed to adjust consistency)
- 2 tablespoons chopped fresh cilantro (for garnish)
- 2 green onions, thinly sliced (for garnish)
- Crushed peanuts (for garnish, optional)

Instructions:
1. Cook the noodles according to the package instructions until al dente. Drain and rinse under cold water to stop the cooking process. Set aside.
2. In a medium bowl, whisk together the peanut butter, soy sauce, rice vinegar, sesame oil, honey or maple syrup, lime juice, minced garlic, grated ginger, and red pepper flakes until smooth. If the sauce is too thick, gradually add water, 1 tablespoon at a time, until you reach your desired consistency. Set aside.
3. Heat a large skillet or wok over medium heat. Add the cooked noodles to the skillet along with the prepared peanut sauce.
4. Toss the noodles and sauce together until the noodles are evenly coated and heated through, about 2-3 minutes. If the noodles seem too dry, you can add a little more water to loosen the sauce.
5. Once heated through, remove the skillet from the heat. Taste and adjust seasoning if needed, adding more soy sauce, lime juice, or red pepper flakes as desired.
6. Transfer the Thai peanut noodles to serving plates or bowls. Garnish with chopped fresh cilantro, sliced green onions, and crushed peanuts (if using).
7. Serve the noodles immediately, and enjoy!

Feel free to customize this recipe by adding your favorite vegetables, such as bell peppers, carrots, or snow peas, or protein, such as cooked chicken, tofu, or shrimp. The peanut sauce is very versatile and pairs well with a variety of ingredients!

BBQ Chicken Pizza

BBQ Chicken Pizza

Ingredients:
- 1 pre-made pizza crust or homemade pizza dough
- 1/2 cup barbecue sauce (homemade or store-bought)
- 1 cup cooked chicken breast, shredded or diced
- 1 cup shredded mozzarella cheese
- 1/2 red onion, thinly sliced
- 1/4 cup fresh cilantro leaves, chopped (optional)
- Olive oil, for brushing
- Cornmeal or flour, for dusting (if using homemade dough)

Instructions:
1. Preheat your oven to the temperature specified for your pizza crust or dough.
2. If using homemade pizza dough, roll it out on a lightly floured surface to your desired thickness. Transfer the dough to a pizza pan or baking sheet that has been lightly dusted with cornmeal or flour.
3. Brush the pizza dough with a thin layer of olive oil. This will help prevent the crust from getting soggy.
4. Spread the barbecue sauce evenly over the oiled pizza crust, leaving a small border around the edges for the crust.
5. Sprinkle the shredded chicken evenly over the barbecue sauce.
6. Scatter the sliced red onion over the chicken.
7. Sprinkle the shredded mozzarella cheese evenly over the pizza.
8. If desired, sprinkle chopped fresh cilantro leaves over the top for extra flavor.
9. Place the pizza in the preheated oven and bake according to the instructions for your pizza crust or dough, or until the crust is golden brown and the cheese is melted and bubbly.
10. Once done, remove the pizza from the oven and let it cool for a few minutes before slicing.
11. Slice the BBQ chicken pizza into wedges or squares, and serve hot. Enjoy!

Feel free to customize this pizza with additional toppings such as sliced bell peppers, diced tomatoes, jalapeños, or cooked bacon. You can also use a combination of different cheeses, such as cheddar, Monterey Jack, or Gouda, to suit your taste preferences.

Veggie Burrito Bowl

Veggie Burrito Bowl

Ingredients:
For the Rice:
- 1 cup white or brown rice
- 2 cups water
- Salt to taste

For the Beans:
- 1 can (15 oz) black beans, drained and rinsed
- 1 teaspoon ground cumin
- 1 teaspoon chili powder
- Salt to taste

For the Veggie Mix:
- 1 tablespoon olive oil
- 1 onion, diced
- 2 bell peppers (any color), diced
- 1 cup corn kernels (fresh, frozen, or canned)
- 1 teaspoon ground cumin
- 1 teaspoon chili powder
- Salt and pepper to taste

For the Toppings:
- Sliced avocado or guacamole
- Chopped fresh cilantro
- Salsa or pico de gallo
- Sour cream or Greek yogurt (optional)
- Lime wedges
- Shredded cheese (such as cheddar or Monterey Jack)

Instructions:
Cooking the Rice:
1. Rinse the rice under cold water until the water runs clear.
2. In a medium saucepan, combine the rinsed rice, water, and salt. Bring to a boil over high heat.
3. Reduce the heat to low, cover, and simmer for about 18-20 minutes, or until the rice is tender and the water is absorbed.
4. Remove from heat and let it sit, covered, for 5 minutes. Fluff the rice with a fork.

Preparing the Beans:
1. In a small saucepan, combine the black beans, ground cumin, chili powder, and a pinch of salt.
2. Heat over medium heat until warmed through, stirring occasionally. Keep warm.

Cooking the Veggie Mix:
1. Heat the olive oil in a large skillet over medium heat.
2. Add the diced onion and sauté for 2-3 minutes until softened.
3. Add the diced bell peppers and corn kernels to the skillet. Cook for another 5-7 minutes, or until the vegetables are tender.
4. Season the veggie mix with ground cumin, chili powder, salt, and pepper. Stir to combine.

Assembling the Burrito Bowls:
1. Divide the cooked rice among serving bowls.
2. Top each bowl with the seasoned black beans and veggie mix.
3. Add your desired toppings such as sliced avocado or guacamole, chopped cilantro, salsa or pico de gallo, sour cream or Greek yogurt, lime wedges, and shredded cheese.
4. Serve immediately and enjoy your veggie burrito bowls!

Feel free to customize this recipe by adding other toppings like diced tomatoes, sliced jalapeños, or shredded lettuce. You can also add protein such as grilled tofu, seasoned tempeh, or grilled chicken if desired.

Mushroom Risotto

Mushroom Risotto

Ingredients:
- 1 1/2 cups Arborio rice
- 4 cups vegetable or chicken broth
- 1/2 cup dry white wine (optional)
- 2 tablespoons olive oil
- 2 tablespoons unsalted butter
- 1 onion, finely chopped
- 2 cloves garlic, minced
- 8 oz (225g) mushrooms (such as cremini, shiitake, or button), sliced
- 1/2 cup grated Parmesan cheese
- Salt and pepper to taste
- Chopped fresh parsley or thyme for garnish (optional)

Instructions:
1. In a saucepan, heat the vegetable or chicken broth over medium heat. Keep it warm while you prepare the risotto.
2. In a large skillet or pot, heat the olive oil and butter over medium heat. Add the chopped onion and cook until softened, about 3-4 minutes. Add the minced garlic and cook for an additional minute, until fragrant.
3. Add the sliced mushrooms to the skillet and cook, stirring occasionally, until they are golden brown and tender, about 5-7 minutes. Season with salt and pepper to taste.
4. Add the Arborio rice to the skillet and stir to coat the grains with the oil and butter. Cook for 1-2 minutes, until the rice is lightly toasted.
5. If using, pour in the dry white wine and stir until it has been absorbed by the rice.
6. Begin adding the warm broth to the skillet, one ladleful at a time, stirring frequently. Allow each addition of broth to be absorbed by the rice before adding more. Continue this process until the rice is creamy and cooked to al dente, about 18-20 minutes.
7. Once the rice is cooked, remove the skillet from the heat. Stir in the grated Parmesan cheese until melted and well combined.
8. Taste the risotto and adjust seasoning with salt and pepper if needed.
9. Serve the mushroom risotto hot, garnished with chopped fresh parsley or thyme if desired.
10. Enjoy your creamy and flavorful mushroom risotto as a comforting meal or a side dish!

Feel free to customize this recipe by adding other ingredients like spinach, peas, or roasted garlic for additional flavor and texture. You can also experiment with different types of mushrooms to vary the flavor profile of the risotto.

Sautéed Garlic Butter Shrimp

Sautéed Garlic Butter Shrimp

Ingredients:
- 1 pound (450g) large shrimp, peeled and deveined
- 3 tablespoons unsalted butter
- 3 cloves garlic, minced
- 1 tablespoon lemon juice
- Salt and pepper to taste
- Chopped fresh parsley for garnish
- Optional: Crushed red pepper flakes for a bit of heat

Instructions:
1. Pat the shrimp dry with paper towels and season them with salt and pepper to taste.
2. In a large skillet, melt the butter over medium heat.
3. Add the minced garlic to the skillet and sauté for about 1 minute, or until fragrant.
4. Add the seasoned shrimp to the skillet in a single layer. Cook for 1-2 minutes on each side, or until the shrimp are pink and opaque.
5. Once the shrimp are cooked through, add the lemon juice to the skillet and stir to combine. This will deglaze the pan and incorporate any flavorful bits stuck to the bottom.
6. Taste the shrimp and adjust seasoning with salt and pepper if needed. If you like a bit of heat, you can also sprinkle some crushed red pepper flakes over the shrimp at this point.
7. Once done, remove the skillet from the heat and transfer the garlic butter shrimp to a serving platter.
8. Garnish the shrimp with chopped fresh parsley for a pop of color and flavor.
9. Serve the sautéed garlic butter shrimp hot, either on its own as an appetizer or over cooked pasta, rice, or salad greens for a main course.
10. Enjoy your flavorful and buttery shrimp dish!

Feel free to customize this recipe by adding other seasonings or herbs such as chopped fresh thyme or rosemary. You can also add a splash of white wine or chicken broth to the skillet along with the lemon juice for extra flavor.

Turkey Chili

Turkey Chili

Ingredients:
- 1 tablespoon olive oil
- 1 onion, chopped
- 3 cloves garlic, minced
- 1 bell pepper, diced
- 1 pound (450g) ground turkey
- 2 tablespoons chili powder
- 1 teaspoon ground cumin
- 1 teaspoon dried oregano
- 1/2 teaspoon paprika
- 1/4 teaspoon cayenne pepper (optional, for heat)
- Salt and pepper to taste
- 1 can (14.5 oz) diced tomatoes
- 1 can (15 oz) kidney beans, drained and rinsed
- 1 cup chicken broth or water
- Optional toppings: shredded cheese, chopped fresh cilantro, diced avocado, sour cream, sliced green onions

Instructions:
1. Heat the olive oil in a large pot or Dutch oven over medium heat.
2. Add the chopped onion and diced bell pepper to the pot. Cook, stirring occasionally, until the vegetables are softened, about 5 minutes.
3. Add the minced garlic to the pot and cook for an additional 1-2 minutes, until fragrant.
4. Push the vegetables to the side of the pot and add the ground turkey to the empty space. Cook, breaking up the meat with a spoon, until it is browned and cooked through.
5. Stir the cooked turkey into the vegetables, then add the chili powder, ground cumin, dried oregano, paprika, cayenne pepper (if using), salt, and pepper. Cook for 1-2 minutes, until the spices are fragrant.
6. Pour in the diced tomatoes (with their juices), drained and rinsed kidney beans, and chicken broth or water. Stir to combine everything evenly.
7. Bring the chili to a simmer, then reduce the heat to low. Cover and let it simmer gently for about 20-30 minutes, stirring occasionally.
8. Taste the chili and adjust seasoning with salt and pepper if needed. If you prefer a thinner consistency, you can add more broth or water.
9. Once the chili is done cooking and the flavors have melded together, remove it from the heat.
10. Serve the turkey chili hot, garnished with your favorite toppings such as shredded cheese, chopped fresh cilantro, diced avocado, sour cream, or sliced green onions.
11. Enjoy your comforting bowl of turkey chili!

Feel free to customize this recipe by adding other ingredients like corn, diced tomatoes with green chilies, or different types of beans. Adjust the level of heat by increasing or decreasing the amount of chili powder and cayenne pepper to suit your taste preferences.

Falafel with Tzatziki Sauce

Falafel with Tzatziki Sauce

Ingredients:
For the Falafel:
- 1 can (15 oz) chickpeas, drained and rinsed
- 1/2 cup chopped fresh parsley
- 1/4 cup chopped fresh cilantro
- 1/2 onion, chopped
- 3 cloves garlic, minced
- 1 teaspoon ground cumin
- 1 teaspoon ground coriander
- 1/2 teaspoon paprika
- 1/4 teaspoon cayenne pepper (optional, for heat)
- Salt and pepper to taste
- 2-3 tablespoons all-purpose flour or chickpea flour (for binding)
- Vegetable oil for frying

For the Tzatziki Sauce:
- 1 cup plain Greek yogurt
- 1/2 cucumber, grated and squeezed to remove excess moisture
- 1-2 cloves garlic, minced
- 1 tablespoon freshly squeezed lemon juice
- 1 tablespoon chopped fresh dill (or 1 teaspoon dried dill)
- Salt and pepper to taste

Instructions:
For the Falafel:
1. In a food processor, combine the chickpeas, chopped parsley, chopped cilantro, chopped onion, minced garlic, ground cumin, ground coriander, paprika, cayenne pepper (if using), salt, and pepper. Pulse until the mixture is finely chopped but not completely smooth.
2. Transfer the falafel mixture to a bowl. Add 2 tablespoons of flour and mix well. If the mixture is too wet, add an additional tablespoon of flour as needed until the mixture holds together when shaped into balls.
3. Shape the falafel mixture into small balls or patties, about 1 1/2 inches in diameter.
4. Heat vegetable oil in a large skillet over medium-high heat. Carefully add the falafel to the hot oil in batches, making sure not to overcrowd the skillet.
5. Fry the falafel for 2-3 minutes on each side, or until golden brown and crispy. Use a slotted spoon to transfer the cooked falafel to a plate lined with paper towels to drain excess oil.

For the Tzatziki Sauce:
1. In a bowl, combine the Greek yogurt, grated cucumber, minced garlic, lemon juice, chopped fresh dill, salt, and pepper. Stir until well combined.
2. Taste the tzatziki sauce and adjust seasoning with salt and pepper if needed. If you prefer a thinner consistency, you can add a splash of water or olive oil.
3. Cover the tzatziki sauce and refrigerate for at least 30 minutes to allow the flavors to meld together.

Serving:
1. Serve the falafel hot, garnished with fresh herbs if desired, and accompanied by the tzatziki sauce for dipping or drizzling.
2. Enjoy your delicious homemade falafel with creamy tzatziki sauce!

Feel free to serve the falafel in pita bread with lettuce, tomato, and onion for a classic falafel sandwich, or serve it over a salad or rice for a lighter meal.

Hawaiian Chicken Skewers

Hawaiian Chicken Skewers

Ingredients:
For the Chicken Skewers:
- 1 1/2 pounds (680g) boneless, skinless chicken breasts or thighs, cut into bite-sized pieces
- 1 bell pepper, cut into chunks
- 1 red onion, cut into chunks
- Pineapple chunks (fresh or canned)

For the Marinade:
- 1/2 cup pineapple juice
- 1/4 cup soy sauce
- 2 tablespoons ketchup
- 2 tablespoons brown sugar
- 2 cloves garlic, minced
- 1 teaspoon grated ginger
- 1 tablespoon vegetable oil
- Salt and pepper to taste

For Garnish (optional):
- Chopped green onions
- Sesame seeds

For Skewers:
- Wooden or metal skewers (if using wooden skewers, soak them in water for 30 minutes before using to prevent burning)

Instructions:
1. In a bowl, whisk together all the marinade ingredients: pineapple juice, soy sauce, ketchup, brown sugar, minced garlic, grated ginger, vegetable oil, salt, and pepper.
2. Place the chicken pieces in a shallow dish or resealable plastic bag. Pour the marinade over the chicken, making sure it's evenly coated. Cover the dish or seal the bag and marinate in the refrigerator for at least 30 minutes, or up to 4 hours. The longer you marinate, the more flavorful the chicken will be.
3. Preheat your grill to medium-high heat.
4. While the grill is heating, thread the marinated chicken pieces, bell pepper chunks, red onion chunks, and pineapple chunks onto the skewers, alternating between them.
5. Once the grill is hot, lightly oil the grates to prevent sticking. Place the skewers on the grill and cook for about 8-10 minutes, turning occasionally, or until the chicken is cooked through and the vegetables are tender and slightly charred.
6. While grilling, you can baste the skewers with any remaining marinade for extra flavor.
7. Once done, remove the skewers from the grill and transfer them to a serving platter.
8. Garnish the Hawaiian chicken skewers with chopped green onions and sesame seeds, if desired.
9. Serve the skewers hot with rice or quinoa and your favorite side dishes.
10. Enjoy your delicious Hawaiian chicken skewers with family and friends!

Feel free to customize this recipe by adding other vegetables like cherry tomatoes or zucchini to the skewers. You can also adjust the sweetness by adding more or less brown sugar to the marinade, according to your taste preferences.

Beef and Broccoli Stir-Fry

Beef and Broccoli Stir-Fry

Ingredients:
For the Stir-Fry Sauce:
- 1/4 cup soy sauce
- 2 tablespoons oyster sauce
- 1 tablespoon brown sugar
- 1 tablespoon rice vinegar
- 1 teaspoon sesame oil
- 2 cloves garlic, minced
- 1 teaspoon grated ginger
- 1 tablespoon cornstarch mixed with 2 tablespoons water (to thicken the sauce)
- 1/4 cup water or beef broth (optional, for a thinner sauce)

For the Stir-Fry:
- 1 pound (450g) flank steak or sirloin, thinly sliced against the grain
- 2 tablespoons vegetable oil, divided
- 1 head broccoli, cut into florets
- 1 onion, thinly sliced
- Cooked rice or noodles, for serving
- Sesame seeds and sliced green onions, for garnish (optional)

Instructions:
For the Stir-Fry Sauce:
1. In a small bowl, whisk together the soy sauce, oyster sauce, brown sugar, rice vinegar, sesame oil, minced garlic, and grated ginger until well combined.
2. In a separate small bowl, mix the cornstarch with water until smooth. This will be used to thicken the sauce later.
3. If you prefer a thinner sauce, you can add 1/4 cup of water or beef broth to the sauce mixture. Set aside.

For the Stir-Fry:
1. Heat 1 tablespoon of vegetable oil in a large skillet or wok over high heat.
2. Add the sliced beef to the hot skillet in a single layer. Cook for 1-2 minutes without stirring, allowing it to sear and develop a nice crust.
3. Stir-fry the beef for an additional 1-2 minutes until it is browned but still slightly pink in the center. Transfer the cooked beef to a plate and set aside.
4. In the same skillet, add the remaining tablespoon of vegetable oil. Add the broccoli florets and sliced onion to the skillet. Stir-fry for 3-4 minutes, or until the vegetables are tender-crisp.
5. Return the cooked beef to the skillet with the vegetables. Give the stir-fry sauce a quick stir, then pour it over the beef and vegetables in the skillet.
6. Cook, stirring constantly, for 1-2 minutes until the sauce has thickened and everything is evenly coated.
7. Taste and adjust seasoning with salt and pepper if needed.
8. Once done, remove the skillet from the heat.

Serving:
1. Serve the beef and broccoli stir-fry hot over cooked rice or noodles.
2. Garnish with sesame seeds and sliced green onions, if desired.
3. Enjoy your delicious homemade beef and broccoli stir-fry!

Feel free to customize this recipe by adding other vegetables like bell peppers, snap peas, or carrots. You can also adjust the level of heat by adding crushed red pepper flakes or chili paste to the stir-fry sauce.

Sweet Potato and Black Bean Quesadillas

Sweet Potato and Black Bean Quesadillas

Ingredients:
- 2 medium sweet potatoes, peeled and diced
- 1 can (15 oz) black beans, drained and rinsed
- 1 red bell pepper, diced
- 1 small onion, diced
- 2 cloves garlic, minced
- 1 teaspoon ground cumin
- 1 teaspoon chili powder
- Salt and pepper to taste
- 1 cup shredded cheese (such as cheddar, Monterey Jack, or a Mexican blend)
- 4 large flour tortillas
- Olive oil or cooking spray
- Optional toppings: avocado slices, salsa, sour cream, chopped cilantro

Instructions:
1. Preheat your oven to 400°F (200°C).
2. Place the diced sweet potatoes on a baking sheet. Drizzle with olive oil and sprinkle with salt and pepper. Toss to coat evenly.
3. Roast the sweet potatoes in the preheated oven for 20-25 minutes, or until tender and slightly caramelized. Remove from the oven and set aside.
4. In a skillet, heat a drizzle of olive oil over medium heat. Add the diced onion and red bell pepper. Cook for 3-4 minutes, or until softened.
5. Add the minced garlic, ground cumin, and chili powder to the skillet. Cook for an additional 1-2 minutes, until fragrant.
6. Add the black beans to the skillet, along with the roasted sweet potatoes. Stir to combine and cook for another 2-3 minutes to heat everything through. Season with salt and pepper to taste. Remove from heat.
7. Heat a separate skillet or griddle over medium heat. Place a flour tortilla on the skillet.
8. Spoon some of the sweet potato and black bean mixture onto half of the tortilla. Sprinkle with shredded cheese. Fold the other half of the tortilla over the filling to create a quesadilla.
9. Cook the quesadilla for 2-3 minutes on each side, or until golden brown and crispy, and the cheese is melted.
10. Repeat with the remaining tortillas and filling ingredients.
11. Once done, remove the quesadillas from the skillet and let them cool for a minute before slicing into wedges.
12. Serve the sweet potato and black bean quesadillas hot, with optional toppings such as avocado slices, salsa, sour cream, or chopped cilantro.
13. Enjoy your delicious and nutritious quesadillas!

Feel free to customize this recipe by adding other ingredients such as corn, diced tomatoes, or green chilies to the filling. You can also use whole wheat or spinach tortillas for added fiber and nutrients.

Chicken Piccata

Chicken Piccata

Ingredients:
- 4 boneless, skinless chicken breasts
- Salt and pepper to taste
- 1/2 cup all-purpose flour, for dredging
- 4 tablespoons unsalted butter, divided
- 2 tablespoons olive oil
- 1/3 cup fresh lemon juice (about 2 lemons)
- 1/2 cup chicken broth
- 1/4 cup brined capers, rinsed and drained
- 1/4 cup chopped fresh parsley, for garnish
- Lemon slices, for garnish

Instructions:
1. Place each chicken breast between two sheets of plastic wrap and gently pound them to an even thickness, about 1/2 inch. Season both sides of the chicken breasts with salt and pepper.
2. Dredge each chicken breast in the flour, shaking off any excess.
3. In a large skillet, heat 2 tablespoons of butter and the olive oil over medium-high heat.
4. Add the chicken breasts to the skillet and cook for about 3-4 minutes on each side, or until golden brown and cooked through. Remove the chicken from the skillet and transfer to a plate. Cover with foil to keep warm.
5. In the same skillet, add the lemon juice, chicken broth, and capers. Bring to a boil, scraping up any browned bits from the bottom of the skillet.
6. Let the sauce simmer for 5 minutes, or until slightly reduced.
7. Stir in the remaining 2 tablespoons of butter until melted and the sauce has thickened slightly.
8. Return the chicken breasts to the skillet, turning them to coat in the sauce. Cook for an additional minute to heat through.
9. Once done, remove the skillet from the heat.
10. Garnish the chicken piccata with chopped fresh parsley and lemon slices.
11. Serve the chicken piccata hot, with additional sauce spooned over the top if desired.
12. Enjoy your delicious and flavorful chicken piccata!

Feel free to serve chicken piccata with pasta, rice, or mashed potatoes, and your favorite vegetables on the side. This dish pairs well with a crisp white wine such as Pinot Grigio or Sauvignon Blanc.

Veggie Frittata

Veggie Frittata

Ingredients:
- 8 large eggs
- 1/4 cup milk or heavy cream
- Salt and pepper to taste
- 1 tablespoon olive oil
- 1 small onion, diced
- 1 bell pepper, diced
- 1 cup sliced mushrooms
- 1 cup baby spinach leaves
- 1/2 cup cherry tomatoes, halved
- 1/2 cup shredded cheese (such as cheddar, mozzarella, or feta)
- Fresh herbs for garnish (optional)

Instructions:
1. Preheat your oven to 350°F (175°C).
2. In a large bowl, whisk together the eggs, milk or heavy cream, salt, and pepper until well combined. Set aside.
3. Heat the olive oil in an oven-safe skillet (such as a cast iron skillet) over medium heat.
4. Add the diced onion and bell pepper to the skillet. Cook for 3-4 minutes, or until softened.
5. Add the sliced mushrooms to the skillet and cook for another 3-4 minutes, or until they release their moisture and start to brown.
6. Add the baby spinach leaves to the skillet and cook for 1-2 minutes, or until wilted.
7. Pour the egg mixture into the skillet, covering the vegetables evenly.
8. Arrange the halved cherry tomatoes on top of the egg mixture, cut side up.
9. Sprinkle the shredded cheese evenly over the top of the frittata.
10. Transfer the skillet to the preheated oven and bake for 15-20 minutes, or until the frittata is set in the center and the edges are golden brown.
11. Once done, remove the skillet from the oven and let the frittata cool for a few minutes.
12. Garnish the veggie frittata with fresh herbs, if desired.
13. Slice the frittata into wedges and serve hot or at room temperature.
14. Enjoy your delicious and nutritious veggie frittata!

Feel free to customize this recipe by using your favorite vegetables or adding cooked potatoes, diced ham, or crumbled bacon for extra flavor. You can also experiment with different herbs and cheeses to suit your taste preferences.

Printed in Great Britain
by Amazon